THA...

A FAMILY IN ROA...

RG41 3HT

...roduced
...t of

ISBN 0 9510739 6 6

Acknowledgements

This volume, being one in a series researched over a period of some 30 years, includes numerous contributions from too many sources to name.

However, of particular significance has been the assistance given by former 'Thackray's Way' employees Nobby Earley, Lionel Godsell, Bob Jackman and Ted Franklin. Other local Reading area contacts have included Joe Challis, Ray Doddington, T.J.G. Homer and Edgar Jordan, who are thanked for sharing their firsthand recollections.

From within enthusiast circles I would like to thank Dave Jones of the Gilford Register, Chris Taylor of the Omnibus Society, Roger Atkinson of the Transport Ticket Society, Alan Townsin, Reg Westgate of H.J. Publications, Peter Jaques of the Kithead Trust and various members of the London Vintage Taxi Association. Also, the various photographers, now mostly deceased, without whose forethought in the recording of events this story would have been less comprehensive.

A fuller appreciation of the Thackray families and their business ventures has only been made possible by the invaluable contributions of family members. In this respect I would like to thank the late Vera Allen (daughter of Bob Thackray), Ray Thackray (daughter of Joe Thackray), Colin Davies (grandson of Herbert Syms), Diana Bradley (cousin of Colin Davies), Brian Thackray (son of Fred Thackray), Lily Steel (daughter of George Thackray) and Stephen Saunders (grandson of Bob Thackray).

I would also like to thank the staff of the Local Studies Libraries and Local Newspapers in Reading, Newbury, Slough. Maidenhead and Kensington for their assistance and advice. Other references have come from Local Authority Minutes, the Censuses of 1861-1891 and 'Thames Valley' records.

Lastly, but by no means least, I would like to thank John Whitehead, who originally set this project in motion, for making his researches available and for his support and valued suggestions.

Paul Lacey ***September 2001***

The Thackray sons: Left is Bob, with Jim in the centre, Joe on the right and Ben seated. Inset are parents Elizabeth and Joseph.

Contents

Front Cover *is in the colours of the 'Thackray's Way' coaches, together with the hat badge issued to crews.* ***Back cover*** *shows a selection of tickets issued on both the pirate buses and the later coaches. Other items show the types of London bus and motor cabs operated.*

Chapter One The Seeking of Fortunes

Joseph Thackray had arrived in London from the Huntingdonshire village of Godmanchester by 1865. Living at Lupus Street in Pimlico, he was working as a salesman when he married Elizabeth Deighton on 30th April 1865. Her family had been established in that village since the 1500's.

Their daughter Emily was born in Notting Hill in 1866 and, by September 1869, the family were living at 18 Cotsford Mews, Notting Hill. That location had been re-named Thorpe Mews by the following August, when son Benjamin arrived.

During this period Joseph started driving a Hansom cab, probably employed by an owner of such a vehicle, but by April 1871 he had become a cab proprietor in his own right.

Although no photos have come to light of the Thackray hansom cabs, this shot was taken by George Thackray in 1939 of the last of such cabs in use in London. Mr. Cutmore was the driver for owner Patterson of Oxford Gardens and the cab was finally withdrawn after the start of the Blitz.

6 Two other members of Joseph's generation also moved to London, with his brother Edmund becoming a nurseryman in Kensington by 1870. James Thackray, also from the Godmanchester line was a railway signalman in the St. Pancras area by 1881.

At some point between April 1871 and 1872 the family returned to live in Godmanchester, where they ran a dairy and cream cheese manufactury in London Road. The family continued to grow with the arrival of further sons Joseph (1872), Robert (1877) and James Deighton (1880), together with daughters Ellen (1875) and Lizzie (1888).

Unfortunately for Elizabeth, Joseph later left her and the children to seek his fortune in London, making it very difficult to support the growing family on the smallholding. Bob was not much in favour of attending school but, fortunately he was hard-working, astute and ambitious. At 14 years old he was working for his mother as a milk boy. She duly apprenticed him to a blacksmith, but he had other ideas!

Joseph senior returned to the trade of cab proprietor, reputedly living with a music hall artiste. However, he obviously kept in touch with his children, as subsequent events will bear witness.

By the spring of 1891 Ben had left home also for London, where he became the driver of a horse-drawn Hansom cab. He was to spend his whole working life as a London 'cabbie' and was a popular character both in the trade and with his passengers. His favourite saying was 'they used to call me han'som', as a reference to his original mode of transport.

Ben married Charlotte Trumble on 20th September 1897, and at that time both he and his father Joseph were living at 3 Pembridge Mews in West Kensington. Ben and Charlotte had Evelyn Lillie (1898) and Benjamin George (1902). By March 1902 Ben and Charlotte had moved to 7 Tavistock Crescent, which was situated a little further north.

When it came to Bob's turn to leave home the Boer War had started, so he joined the army, enlisting with the Royal Horse Artillery on 13th February 1900. He signed up for one year, but did not see service abroad, instead being posted to Woolwich and Ireland and served as a farrier.

7 When Bob reached the end of his year in the Army he joined Ben in London, driving a Hansom cab until he had saved enough money to buy his own one. Gradually he built up a small fleet of horse-drawn cabs in the early years of the 20th century, also undertaking other Jobmasters work early on.

With the advent of motor cabs in London in 1905 Bob was quick to adopt the new innovation. A pair of cabs was purchased, one driven by himself, and he employed Ben to drive the other. The earliest known examples were Renaults, and more were added from about 1907, confirming the dominance of the French–built chassis as the basis for London cabs at that time.

Ben proudly poses with one of the first Renault motor cabs (LB 6813). Note the 'coal scuttle' arrangement of the bonnet and radiator characteristic of the French chassis. Also note the lack of head-lamps, the oil side lights, the communication tube between passenger and driver and the taximeter on the nearside. Luggage was accommodated beside the driver, who typically continued to wear a uniform associated with the horse-drawn era.

8 The coming of motor cabs to London, starting with just 1 in 1903, was followed by 2 the next year, 19 in 1905, 96 in 1906 up to 723 in 1907. This had a marked effect on the fortunes of the hansom cab owners, with a decline in the number such vehicles from 7,499 to 5,592 during the same period. The larger 4-wheel 'growlers' fared better, partly because of their luggage-carrying capacity, and also because the railway companies banned from motors from the main London termini through fear of fire – a somewhat ironic situation from concerns running coal-burning locomotives throughout the British countryside!

On 26th April 1905 Bob married Alice Palmer at Hythe, by Southampton Water on the fringes of the New Forest. The couple had three children, Edna Lillian (1906), Frederick Robert (1907) and Vera Minnie (1911). Bob had always been the most business-minded member of the family, and duly became the natural head of the expanding enterprise. By January 1907 Bob and Alice were living at 93 Shirland Avenue, just north of Harrow Road and near Paddington Station.

The pace of change on the London cab scene had increased still further, giving a distinct advantage to those who had acquainted themselves with the new mode of propulsion. 2805 motor cabs were on the road in 1908, rising to 6397 by 1910. That was the first year when motors outnumbered hansoms, now down to 4724, and the outmoded vehicles were being sold off at £1 each – many ending up as firewood!

Brother Joe was apprenticed to a carpenter by 1891, but duly joined them in London, as did Jim a little later on. When it had come to Jim's turn to leave Godmanchester, he had initially gone to Boston in Lincolnshire. There he met his wife Ray, and the couple decided to emigrate to Canada in 1908, where he tried his hand at mining, as a black-smith and other work. With the outbreak of the Great War Jim, like many other British emigrants, joined the Canadian Army. He was posted to the Western Front, so his wife returned to Boston, where at least he could visit her when on leave. Their daughter Ray was born at Boston in 1918, and fortunately Jim survived the conflict.

The intention had been for the family to return to Canada, but with the steady expansion of the taxi business Bob offered Jim a job as manager of the business. Jim later became a partner in that and other businesses with

9 Bob, though generally in a more junior capacity as it was Bob who had the real talent for making money.

One of the Thackray daughters Ellen ('Nell') had also followed the brothers to London after working from home as a dressmaker, becoming a schoolmistress in Northolt, Middlesex. Even this had a bearing on the fortunes of the business, as in 1904 she married Herbert Syms, an established motor engineer who had been apprenticed as a carriage-builder.

From 1913 the partnership of 'Thackray & Syms' is evident under the heading of motor car garage proprietors at 13a Colville Mews, and a sizeable building was constructed over the much of the western end of the yard area. A motor car agency was also listed at 14a Colville Mews by the partners from about 1915. By the following year 14 Ledbury Mews West had been added to the advertised premises which we will shortly hear more of as the new base for the growing cab fleet.

However, circa 1919, a somewhat acrimonious split occurred in the partnership, with the result that Bob Thackray and Herbert Syms went their own ways. Apparently, the two men never spoke to each other again.

Syms took over premises in Star Road, Fulham, which had been a cab-operating base since at least 1909. From there he operated a fleet of taxis, with a lion-and-unicorn crest, together with a steam-driven removal lorry.

His daughter Gwen married into the James family, who had a timber yard at Hayes Bridge Wharf They employed several of Syms's redundant Unic taxis for towing work around the yard – one ending its days by being accidentally driven into the canal!

Nell and Herbert Syms moved into 2 Highlever Road, North Kensington when it was new, and later is was sold to her brother Ben. Syms retired in 1944 and the Star Road premises were sold to became the factory for 'Less Toothpaste'.

Herbert Syms had experimented with electrically-propelled cabs, and was instrumental in producing what was acknowledged as the first truly accurate taximeter. This was an important development for taxicab operators, and in recognition of the same Herbert was presented with a canteen of cutlery by the London Motor Cab Proprietors Association in 1916. The meters were manufactured by the 'Geecen' company off the Marylebone Road in London, and Herbert was later succeeded by his daughter Gwen as a director following his death in 1963.

As regards Thackray's own premises, the earliest known are those in Colville Mews, where the horse-drawn cabs and horses were kept around the turn of the century. These duly became inadequate, and a large collection of mews stables and open yard had been obtained at Ledbury Mews West.

This had served as a horse-bus depot for the 'London General Omnibus Co. Ltd.' from 1866 until 1910, and was reached either through an archway adjacent to the 'Ledbury Arms' in Ledbury Road or from Westbourne Grove and via Lambton Place.

In addition the mews had previous been used around 1892 by other cab proprietors William Targett and Robert Kew, but it is not known if these businesses were actually acquired by the Thackrays. Initially the taxis were parked in the old mews stables or in the open, but much of the yard was duly covered with a substantial brick-built garage. An exit through the rear of the garage was maintained into Lambton Place and Westbourne Grove, though it was very narrow and therefore 'one-way' only. Other property was held a little to the north-west at 16 Colville Road and 13a Colville Mews, from which a hire-car and 24-hour general garage business was run. It is worth noting that Robert Kew and his son, also a cabman, had relocated to properties in Colville Road and Colville Mews by 1897, and both were still there in 1905.

The yard area at Ledbury Mews West was expanded before 1914, taking in some of the plot formerly occupied by Edmund Thackray's nursery in Denbigh Road. The latter had relocated to nearby Norfolk Road by 1891, where he and his growing family ran a florist's shop, though the original site may have continued in use in connection with that venture for a time.

During the course of acquiring suitable premises for the above ventures, Bob also had the opportunity to purchase other mews properties nearby in Scampston Mews and Portius Mews, which were his introduction to the property business.

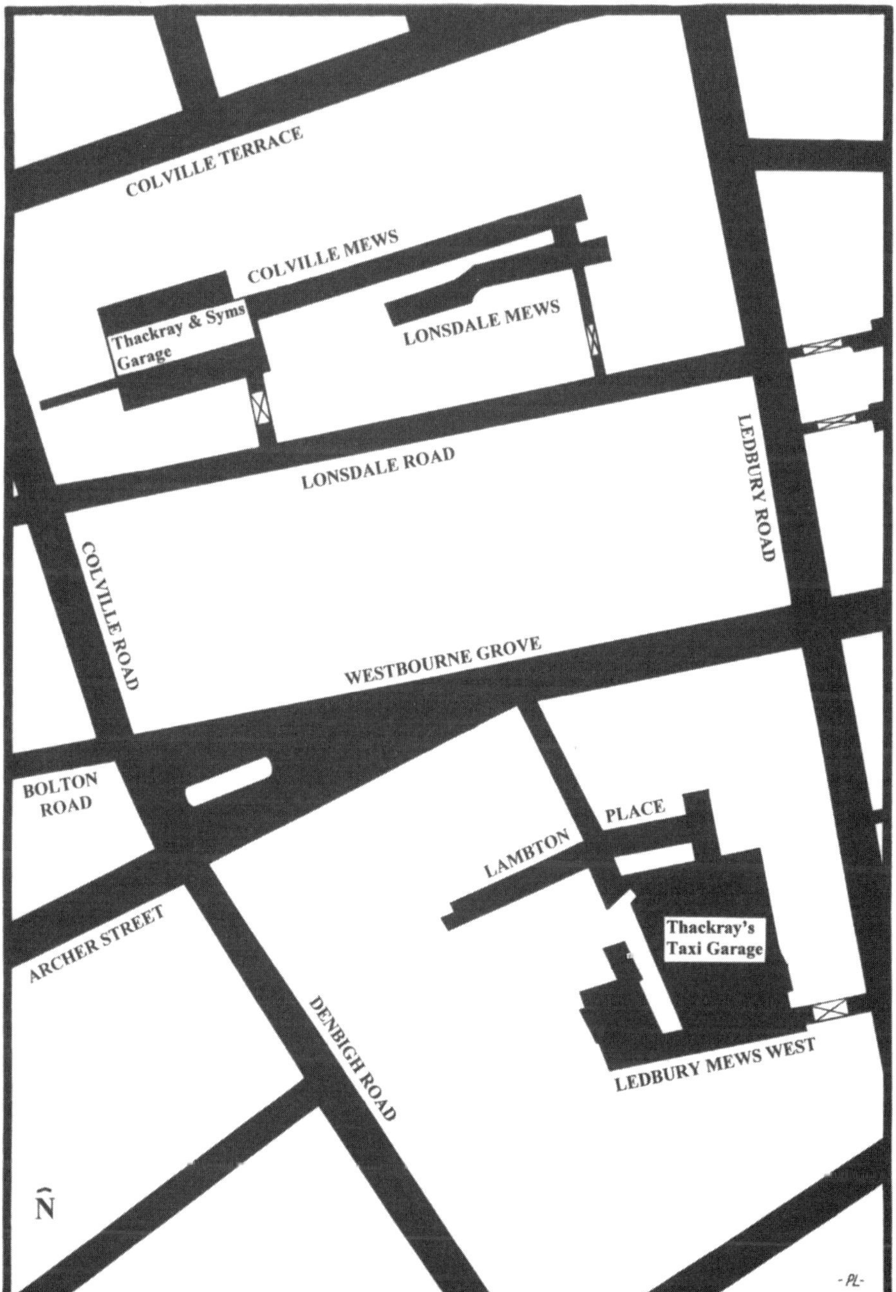
COLVILLE TERRACE
COLVILLE MEWS
Thackray & Syms Garage
LONSDALE MEWS
LONSDALE ROAD
LEDBURY ROAD
COLVILLE ROAD
WESTBOURNE GROVE
BOLTON ROAD
LAMBTON PLACE
Thackray's Taxi Garage
ARCHER STREET
DENBIGH ROAD
LEDBURY MEWS WEST
N
-PL-

By the outbreak of the First World War Bob was living in Caverswall Street, Shepherds Bush, but shortly afterwards he moved into a brand new house in Wembley. However, it had been his desire to have a country property where he could farm a little and his children could have freedoms denied to them in the town. It also needed to be situated conveniently for commuting to his businesses via Paddington, so he came to consider properties in the Reading area. At the end of WW1 the extensive Blagrave Estate at Calcot was being broken up for sale in lots. Bob and Alice were able to purchase Fords Farm and took up residence during 1920.

The farm was situated some three miles west of Reading, 14 miles from Newbury and some 40 miles from central London. It was bounded to the north by the Bath Road and to the south by the Kennet & Avon Canal, each of which has its own place in the annals of transport history. Also representing the nearby railway was his neighbour, in the shape of Sir Felix J. Pole, General Manager of the Great Western Railway.

The rural location very much suited Bob and Alice's children Edna, Vera and Fred, in particular the latter two who were 'horse mad'. It also gave Bob room for relaxation, as he enjoyed playing billiards to the degree that he duly had a room installed for that purpose. He was also interested in both horse and greyhound racing, and by all accounts quite a joker too! He also had a liking for the unusual, including the African monkey parrot he kept as pets. The only disadvantage to the new location was the lack of mains electricity, which was not laid on until many years later.

His interest in racing inevitably led to some involvement with betting and gambling. Bob devised a crest for the doors of his cabs, depicting a cockerel with the motto 'While I Live I'll Crow', a statement that he certainly lived up to! The adopted motif was taken even further on Bob's own car, with a bronze radiator mascot of a cockerel, which survives to this day. However, his brother Jim devised his own alternative, which showed a sitting hen and the legend 'I Deliver The Goods' to grace the cabs he owned!

Bob and his family all became well known in sporting circles, with regular attendance at race meetings etc. Vera duly became a respected horsewoman who achieved success in show jumping at Olympia, whilst her brother Fred became one of the top amateur National Hunt jockeys of his day. Bob rode

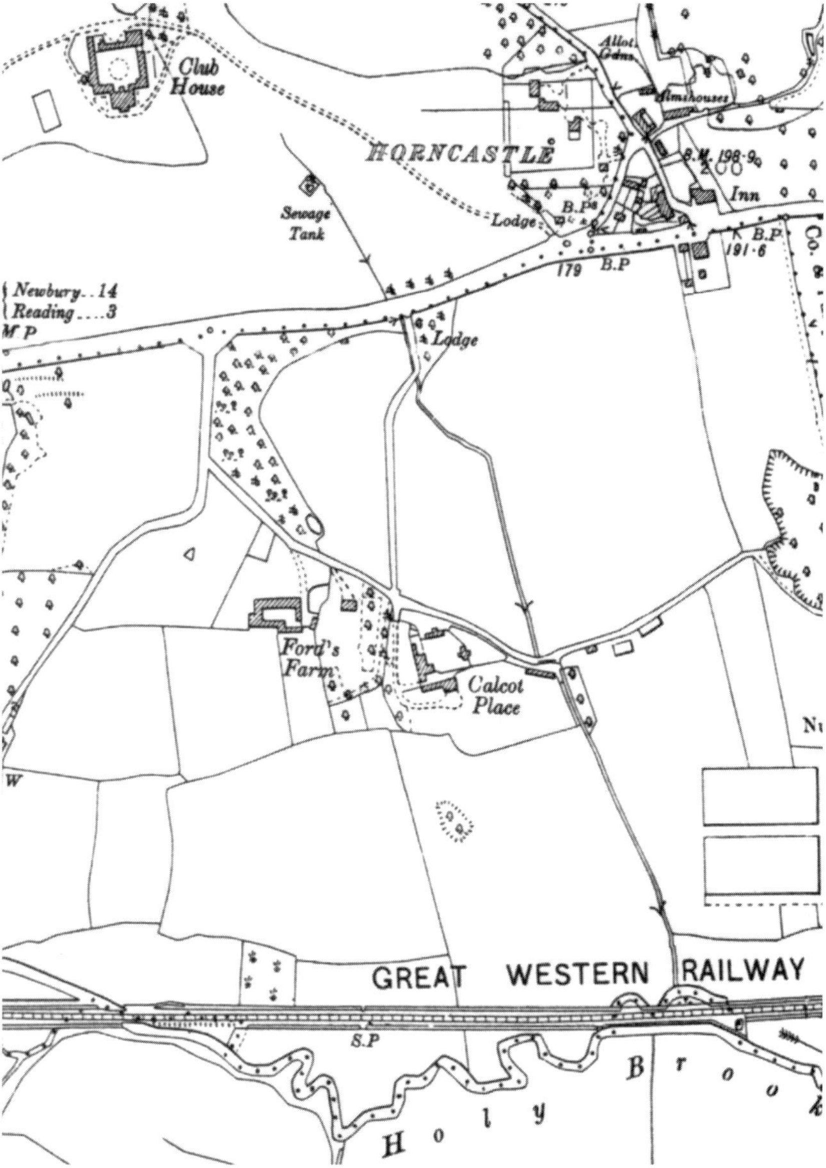

13 *1931 map showing the location of Fords Farm. It was situated very close to the Bath Road, a reminder of the former stage-coach era.*

14 *The farmhouse at Fords Farm, a popular venue for the Thackray family to gather in what was then very rural surroundings.*

himself, and was a keen follower of the nearby South Berks Hunt, and he was also keen on shooting. He was also an accomplished hackney carriage driver and took part in competitions at Olympia and other major equestrian events. Bob was also an active member of the Reading and Smithfield Masonic Lodges. He is also believed to have been a Freeman of both the City of London and Huntingdon.

In view of his relocation to Berkshire, a small office and flat were built at the Ledbury Mews West premises, just to the left of the taxi garage. Use of the Colville Mews did not cease until around 1932.

Chapter Two — Pirate Days

One of the most significant events affecting the history of London's buses in the inter-war years took place on 5th August 1922 and was to attract Bob Thackray's attention as a business opportunity.

On that day Arthur George Partridge (a former taxi driver) had placed in service the first of his 'Chocolate Express' buses, the first of the so-called 'pirate' buses that were to prove a serious challenge to the near monopoly of the 'London General Omnibus Company'. Numerous other operators followed that lead, some with only one bus and others with small fleets. For a decade the streets of London were treated to buses in a wide variety of liveries and bearing many different fleetnames.

Although some order had been imposed on the earlier free-for-all by the London Traffic Act, 1924, which laid down the streets that buses could use, there was still scope for profit to be made.

Having not doubt studied the success of others around him in the streets of West London, Bob decided to become a 'pirate' himself at the end of December 1924. For this venture he took delivery of a quartet of brand new solid-tyred Dennis 4-ton double-deck buses which carried 48-seat, open-top bodies with open rear staircases built by Dodson of Willesden, North London. These bore the registration numbers XW 5567-5570 and were painted in a red and white livery, bearing the fleetname 'Robt. Thackray' in gold script.

Initial operation is believed to have taken place on route 142 (Kilburn Park – Watford), commencing on 3rd January 1925, and the success of the venture can be gauged by the addition of two further identical buses during February 1925, in the shape of XW 68 and XX 906.

During March 1925 Jim Thackray entered into the same line with the purchase of another identical Dennis (XX 3882). Although it was owned by him personally, from an operational standpoint it was regarded as part of an overall Thackray bus fleet. Indeed, it actually carried just the fleetname 'Thackray's' and wore the red and white livery.

16 The pirate buses were housed at the Ledbury Mews West yard, and for a time around 1925-7 some of the vehicles of the 'Premier Omnibus Company' were also stabled there by arrangement. A Mr. H. J. Buchan managed the fleet on a daily basis. Ben's son George came to drive on the buses during this period.

George Thackray with Dennis bus No.5 (XX 3882)

 On 6th January 1926 a limited company under the title 'Robert Thackray Ltd.' was formed. The registered office was at 6 Colville Mews with the whole of the £3000 share capital held by Bob.

In January 1926 a further similar Dennis was added in the shape of YM 4719, and by then the fleet was covering the 15A (Wembley–Strand) and 526D (North Finchley–Wandsworth Bridge) routes. Operation of the latter route was governed by the West London Association, a grouping of independents to which Thackrays belonged, as indeed did 'Birch Bros.'. The arrangement under the Association was for schedules to be drawn up and operators provided the bus and crew to cover its allotted place on the timetable. This was a fairer system than used by some other associations, and contributed to harmonious relations between the various parties. Each operator issued its own tickets and retained all income from journeys covered.

The star shaped badge carried on the sides of buses belonging to the West London Association

During the General Strike of May 1926 the 'Thackray' buses were amongst those which continued to run, with a policeman sat beside the driver to give protection in the volatile atmosphere of the time.

In late 1926 Bob Thackray had been in discussions with 'Birch Bros.' of Kentish Town, who were already experienced bus and cab operators, regarding the joint operation of a new service between Pimlico and

 Hampstead Heath. The route was so devised as to avoid existing services and roads upon which the Metropolitan Police had placed restrictions. However, the application made on 4th November was turned down on the basis that the service crossed too many main roads and would cause inconvenience to traffic.

A further Dennis (YF 5623) was added in May 1927. An attempt was made at some point to allocate fleet numbers to the buses, though only incomplete details have come to light.

Although Bob had looked at ways to expand the bus operations, it soon became evident that the Police attitude to the increasing number of bus proprietors was becoming more stringent.

'Thackray' Dennis No.4 (XW 5667) seen after being sold to 'Public', still on its former 526 service but now bearing fleet number D85.

He therefore decided to sell out his bus business to 'Public', one of the larger 'independents', with effect from 6th October 1927, for £20,300. Five days later Jim also sold out to the same company for £3000. The buses continued to operate out of Ledbury Mews West for their new owner until

23rd May 1928 under a leasing agreement, after which 'Public' reorganised to operate from West Green and Enfield garages. Thackray's former manager Mr. Buchan joined the new owners as manager of the Paddington depot. What the Thackrays (and many others who sold out to that concern) did not know was that the real business behind 'Public' was the 'London General Omnibus Co. Ltd.', who had set it up to acquire as many competitors as possible!

There are no known photos of the numerous Unic cabs operated by Thackray's, but this is another example in London service. Note the arrangements for refuelling, with tanks fixed to the wall and a hand cranked pump.

A little earlier, in January 1928, Elizabeth Thackray passed away at the age of 86.

The taxi business continued to flourish from the Ledbury Mews West base, the fleet of Unic's growing to some 75. As an additional source of income parts of the site were rented out to other firms, with 'Skylark Motor Coaches' being there in 1930/1, followed by a short period from 1st March 1932 by 'London General Country Services' as a base for its 'Green Line' private hire coaches.

Although motor cabs had brought a number of advantages for operators and passengers alike, the period following the First World War also brought its share of difficulties. Between 1917 and 1922 cab fares had achieved only a 12% increase, despite the cost of living having risen by 55%. To make the situation worse, bus and train fares had been allowed to increase by 100% during the same period.

The cost of purchasing cabs themselves had also risen by 50% which, when combined with increases in the cost of Road Tax and Taximeter hire charges, had brought about a crises in the industry. During 1922 that had culminated in a widespread strike by cabmen, though nothing was resolved as a result.

The situation continued to deteriorate throughout the '20's, with the strict rules imposed on the types approved by the Metropolitan Police for use in London not helping the plight of the operators. The growth of bus services, together with the growing numbers of express coaches on the streets of the capital, had made the cab the scapegoat for increased traffic congestion. Indeed, The London Traffic Advisory Committee, charged with sorting out such congestion, made the cabbies plight worse by banning cabs altogether from some streets. In other places traditional cab ranks were replaced by bus layovers.

The suspicion that the LTAC was acting with bias is given credibility when it is noted that it included Frank Pick and Lord Ashfield, the prime figures behind the 'London General Omnibus Co. Ltd.'! Indeed, Ashfield felt strongly that the bus should provide all such journeys, and not be competing with cabs, and in that aspect he found an ally in the Minister of Transport Herbert Morrison.

Chapter Three Enter the Greyhounds

Whilst Bob had been primarily concerned with London bus operation, another transport revolution had its small beginnings on the road that passed his home at Calcot.

The Bath Road had long been associated with the development of road transport, with the long-distance stage-coaches, fast mail-coaches and the coming of the metalled turnpike roadway between London and Bristol. The very first mail-coach had commenced running on that road in 1784, so it was therefore fitting that the same route should also be host to the first daily express motor coach service to be operated.

'Greyhound Motors' took this bold step on 11th February 1925, operating a daily service between its Bristol base and the capital. The coaches were normal control Dennis chassis with well-appointed bodies built by Strachan & Brown of Acton, West London. A single journey was operated in each direction, with each coach leaving Bristol or London (Hammersmith) at 9.00am, with a journey time of 8 hours. The Bristol-London fare was 10 shillings and 6 pence single or £1 return. Intermediate fares were available, with that for Reading to London being 3 shillings and 6 pence for a single or 6 shillings and 6 pence for a return.

In keeping with the stage-coach tradition, passengers left the coach at Newbury to take lunch at the Chequers Hotel, for which 30 minutes was allowed in the timetable. Short 'comfort stops' were also made at the Bear Hotel in Hungerford and the inn of the same name at Maidenhead. It is also worth noting that a regular stop was also made at Cemetery Junction in Reading, where the radiator was topped up if required! Bob Thackray no doubt sampled the new facility, and perhaps it was during such a stop that his attention was drawn to that area of Reading?

The venture was a success and more coaches were added, whilst other operators also started up express coach services on various routes over the next couple of years. A number of those were routed through Reading, all on a general east to west basis using either the Bath or Oxford roads. It should also be appreciated that the railways of the time were not on a particularly popular standing, due to a combination of a pressing need for modernisation and recent rises in fares. The new coach services, run over roads that were still relatively uncluttered with traffic, therefore offered a cleaner alternate with 'first class comforts at third class fares'.

As far as operations through Reading were concerned it was necessary to obtain a hackney carriage licence from the Borough Council if coaches were to pick up or set down in the town. Some local authorities were quite obliging in issuing any licences that were requested. However, as the 1920's drew to a close, the Borough of Reading was becoming much stricter on licensing buses and coaches using the town centre. Officially this was due to congestion in the town centre, though contemporary photographs do not bear this out. It seems that it was rather more a means of keeping the tram routes relatively free of traffic!

AEC 'Renown' HU 4809, with Strachan & Brown of Acton coachwork, was one of the second batch of coaches placed on the Bristol-Newbury-Reading-Maidenhead-London service by 'Greyhound Motors' of Bristol from 27th March 1926. Unlike the solid-tyred Dennis coaches initially used, these had pneumatic tyres from new. Their arrival permitted the doubling of frequency and improved the standard of passenger comfort. The additional departures left from Bristol and London at 11.30am.

23 Despite some reluctance to grant too many licences, the public demand for express coaches led to a steady development of routes passing through the town. The 'Greyhound' coaches were joined from February 1928 by the 'Royal Blue' coaches of Bournemouth-based Elliott Brothers. The latter ran from London to Weston-super-Mare, and the following year saw the appearance of the 'Morning Star' coaches of E. Jones & Son of Bristol.

The arrival of these through services had also been noted by the local 'territorial' bus operator, the Reading-based 'Thames Valley Traction Co. Ltd.', which suddenly decided to start a Reading – London service in May 1927. To some extent the worth of such a venture had been proven by the very popular daily excursions that ran to Wembley during the British Empire Exhibition of 1924-5.

Quite why 'Thames Valley' chose that moment to commence the service is less evident than the fact that initially the Board turned the proposal down in April, only to reverse that decision at the May meeting. However, perhaps as a mark of their scepticism, the service began with only the minimum of resources.

Two of the newly-delivered rear-entrance Brush-bodied Tilling-Stevens B9A's, cars 145/6 (MO 9317/8), were quickly modified for use on the service. Several roof vents were added, together with the fitting of curtains to add some small degree of comfort in their otherwise service saloon bodies.The 'Thames Valley' service ran from Reading (St. Mary's Butts) to London (Lower Belgrave Street, Victoria) via Wokingham, Bracknell, Ascot and Staines. Two journeys ran each day, leaving Reading at 8.15am and 4.30pm, returning from London at 11.00am and 7.00pm. Seats had to be booked in advance and operation of the service required one car only, with 146 being the usual performer.

During May 1928 a pair of Tilling-Stevens B9A's were delivered specifically for the London service. These were cars 159/60 (RX 1394/5), and both carried forward-entrance Brush bodies fitted out to a more luxurious specification. From that month the service was doubled in frequency, with departures from Reading at 815am, 9.30am, 1.45pm and 5.45pm, with returning journeys at 11.00am, 2.00pm, 7.00pm and 8.30pm. The adult return fare was 6 shillings and seats could be booked at various agents along the line of route, those locally also being the TV parcels agencies. In London agents were set up in Hammersmith and Chiswick, including the Hammersmith Road office of the pioneering 'Greyhound Motors'. From April 1929 it also became possible for passengers to book through tickets to destinations all over the country via the 'London Coastal Coaches' agency.

One of the second pair of Tilling Stevens B9A's, 'Thames Valley' car 160 (RX 1395) was added in May 1928. The Brush body was, however, still very bus-like in appearance, not helped by the addition of a destination box during 1929.

Other operators had joined the fray, and by May 1929 Reading's streets daily witnessed the colourful passage of the following services:

'Greyhound' (Bristol)	London – Bristol
	London-Weston-super-Mare
'Morning Star' (Bristol)	London – Bristol
'Royal Blue' (Bournemouth)	London - Weston-super-Mare
'Cook's Safety Coaches' (London)	London - Cardiff/Swansea
'Red Bus' (Gloucester)	London - Gloucester
'Red & White' (Chepstow)	London - Gloucester
'Blue Star' (Gloucester)	London – Gloucester
'Lavender Blue' (Swindon)	London - Swindon

25 The next most significant development came in May 1929, when Ralph Priest of York Road, Kings Cross, London advertised locally his 'Safeway Super Saloon' express coach service between Reading and London. Two coaches worked the route, which ran from Blagrave Street, and both were based somewhere in Reading. As the route chosen ran via the Bath Road through Twyford, Maidenhead and Slough, no clash occurred at first with the TV service. However the fare charged by the newcomer was only 4 shillings for a day return, so the new venture inevitably soon took away a number of through passengers.

The London terminus was Kings Cross and five journeys left Reading at 7.50am, 9.20am, 1.35pm, 5.20pm and 8.35pm, with return journeys at 10.30am, 1.15pm, 6.00pm, 8.45pm and 11.30pm. The latter departure was advertised as a 'theatre coach' and certainly represented a marked improvement over TV's rather early last return journey. Priest was keen to promote the comforts and safety aspects of the Gilford coaches used on the route, and he also developed his own booking agents along the route. Seats were booked in advance and numbered seats could be reserved. The company even undertook to refund the necessary rail fare to any return passenger it found it could not accommodate.

TV reacted to the intruder by improving its own service from Monday 10th June 1929 by out-stationing one of the coaches at the London end. This allowed it to operate six daily journeys departing from Reading at 8.15am, 10.30am, 1.00pm, 2.00pm, 5.00pm and 8.00pm, with return runs at 9.00am, 11.00am, 2.00pm, 4.00pm, 6.00pm and 8.00pm. In order to cover these new schedules the company diverted a trio of Tilling-Stevens B10B2 coaches with well-appointed London Lorries bodies to take the place of 159/60. They were cars 176-8 (RX 4338-40) and had originally been intended for private hire work. It should also be noted that the London terminal point had by then changed to Lupus Street, Pimlico, as a result of traffic congestion in Victoria. 'Safeway' had in fact had to transfer to the nearby Vauxhall Bridge Road not long after commencement for similar reason.

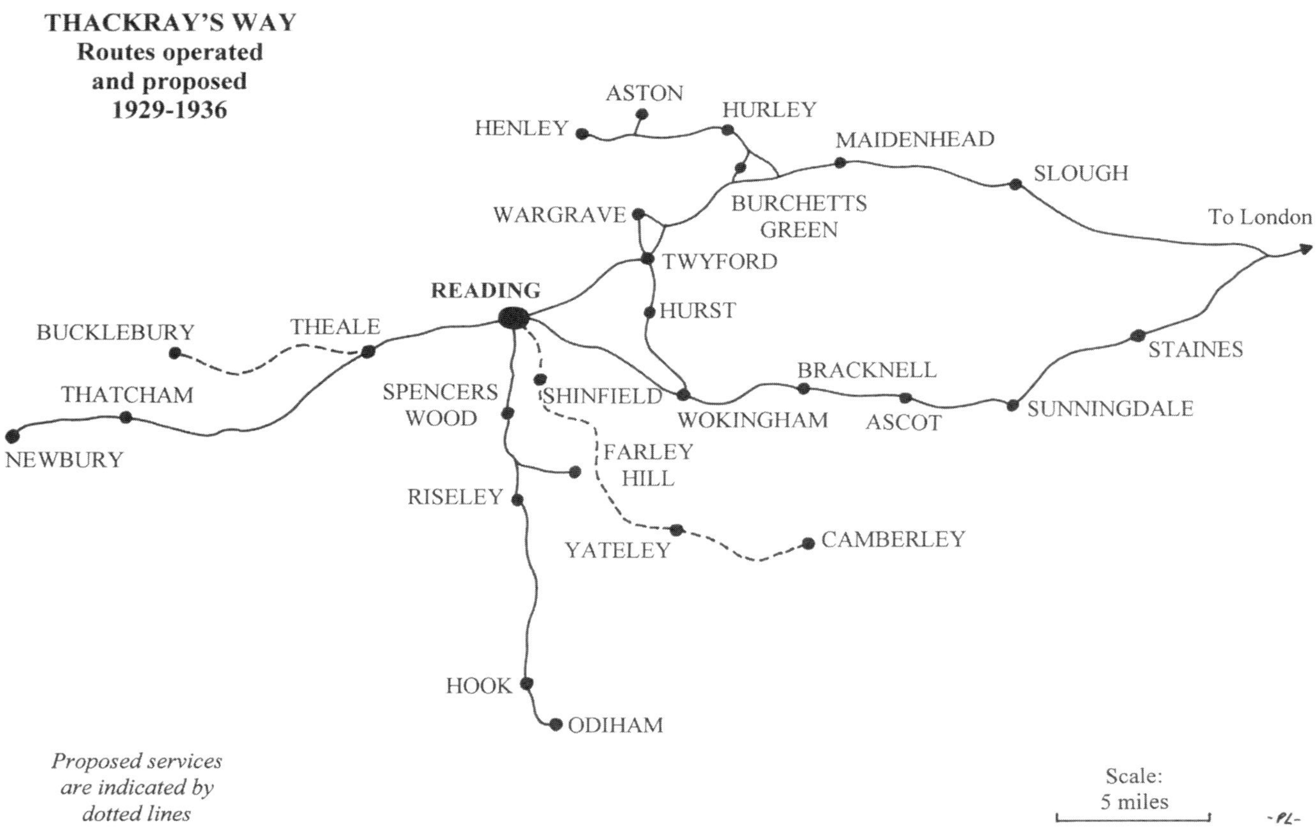
THACKRAY'S WAY
Routes operated
and proposed
1929-1936
HENLEY
ASTON
HURLEY
MAIDENHEAD
SLOUGH
To London
WARGRAVE
BURCHETTS
GREEN
TWYFORD
READING
HURST
BUCKLEBURY
THEALE
STAINES
BRACKNELL
THATCHAM
SPENCERS
WOOD
SHINFIELD
WOKINGHAM
ASCOT
SUNNINGDALE
NEWBURY
FARLEY
HILL
RISELEY
YATELEY
CAMBERLEY
HOOK
ODIHAM
Proposed services
are indicated by
dotted lines
Scale:
5 miles
-PL-

Chapter Four — Into the Fray

All of these developments on the express coach front had not escaped the notice of Bob Thackray, so perhaps it was almost inevitable that he should be tempted to join the fray – particularly as he already possessed a suitable base in London and experience of bus operations!

On 25th July 1929 Robert and James Deighton Thackray were registered as the directors of 'The Ledbury Transport Co. Ltd.', the title for the new venture being inspired by the London taxi base at Ledbury Mews West. The prime objective of the new concern was the operation of an express coach service between Reading and London, but a clash with 'Thames Valley' was largely avoided by the Thackray's decision to use the Bath Road via Twyford, Maidenhead and Slough.

However, the new service had an immediate effect on the 'Safeway' service. The latter found itself forced to try the alternative route via Wokingham, Bracknell, Ascot and Staines, putting it into conflict with the TV operation. Competition between those two concerns kept them busy enough to pay less attention to the Ledbury venture than might have been wise!

Before the new service could commence it was of course necessary to obtain the hackney carriage licenses from Reading Borough Council. In view of Bob and Jim's previous dealings with the licensing authorities in London, it must have come as a relief that the application for 8 licenses was passed without any difficulty when it was dealt with in September 1929.

The initial batch of 6 coaches were fitted with Duple 26-seat dual-doorway bodies finished to a very high standard. These were built on Gilford 166SD chassis, which incorporated such features as four-wheel braking and powerful American-built Lycoming 5.8 litre 6-cylinder engines. These were registered by Duple of Hendon as UV 7962-7, and it has been suggested that they may have initially been leased from the coach-builder. It has been said that not all were in the adopted livery of dark red and cream at first, so they may have indeed been ex-stock rather than built to order. The coaches were delivered in early September and saw some use on excursion work whilst the license application was being sought.

28 Although the company had been formerly named as noted above, the venture was from the outset known as ‘Thackray’s Way’, and that was the fleetname carried along the sides of the smart-looking coaches. Although the choice of name represented a logical progression from that used on the London Dennis buses, it has also been suggested that some ‘mischief’ may have been intended by the superficial similarity with the ‘Thames Valley’ name!

The service is believed to have started on 25th September 1929 with an ambitious hourly headway through from the first departure from Reading at 7.00am until the final return from London at 11.30pm. The adult return fare was set at 4 shillings, thus equalling that charged by ‘Safeway’ and under-cutting that of the ‘Valley’.

The smart new coaches and the frequent timings soon ensured the success of the venture. The ability to work the service from each end was also an important factor, and 2 coaches were kept at the Ledbury Mews site at night. They were actually parked in the yard there and, as room was quite tight, they had to be reversed in from the road and through the archway.

In Reading a temporary solution for housing the fleet was found by using the yard of the long-established garage and coachbuilders William Vincent Ltd. This was situated at their new premises opposite Reading’s two railway stations and had been opened in 1928.

The service also carried a conductor for passenger assistance and to issue tickets. Initially they used punch-type pre-printed tickets, but they were superseded by the original ‘Setright’ insert-type ticket machines, in which ticket blanks were inserted for overprinting with details of the fare and boarding stage by the setting of dials and the turn of a handle. The latter had been introduced to eliminate ‘fiddling’ by the conductors – though many duly became quite adept at dismantling the machines in order to turn back the recording dials!

The Reading terminus was St. Mary’s Butts, with coaches leaving the town via Bridge Street, Southampton Street, Crown Street and the London Road. Tradition was maintained with the days of the stage-coach by the use of ‘The Bear’ in Maidenhead as the main stop in that town.

 The designated London terminus was Oxford Street, though in fact the coaches drew up at 281 Regent Street outside the booking agents 'Highways Ltd.', which was also the main London agent for the company. The service was advertised as 'passing Selfridges and other West End stores', and it also took passengers to within 5 minutes walk of 'Theatreland'. This certainly made it more convenient than either of the competing services for most passengers at the London end.

Gilford coach GC 1871 waits for passengers outside the Oxford Circus Booking Office on a journey bound for Reading.

The 11.30pm 'theatre coach' left Oxford Circus daily (except Sundays), reaching Reading at 1.30am, and having the requirement that seats had to be booked in advance at least 24 hours in advance, and that could be done at a number of booking agents set up along the route.

Well-produced leaflets were a feature of the company from the start, and these duly became replaced by equally informative timetable cards for individual routes and booklets containing all services, the latter supported by commercial advertising.

 On 19th October 1929 'Thackray's Way' announced in the Newbury Weekly News that it was commencing a new link between that town and London. Hackney carriage licences for 8 coaches were granted by Newbury Borough Council a couple of days later, though that authority was far less stringent than Reading, seemingly invoking its rights to exercise such powers only as a source of income.

The precise date for the start of the Newbury link has not been discovered, but it was made possible by the arrival of a further pair of Duple-bodied Gilford 166SD-types in the shape of UW 2615/6 in October. No fleet numbers were carried until much later on, the coaches being known by their registration numerals instead.

This new route was in fact a feeder service, linking with the coaches to and from London at Reading, passengers being required to change coaches there. Through-booking was a feature from the outset, again with agents appointed along the Bath Road. An adult return fare of 6 shillings was offered for the Newbury to London journey.

The initial schedule for the Reading–Newbury link called for a 40-minute frequency, with the first outward coach leaving Reading at 7.00am to form the 8.00am departure from Newbury. With a 55-minute journey time between the two towns each of the three coaches was worked hard, that on the initial run working until 10.55pm with only a total of 75 minutes idle time! Under those arrangements all three coaches were based in Reading, whilst the terminal point in Newbury was in the Market Place.

At the Reading end the coaches approached the town along the Bath Road and thence down Castle Hill and Castle Street to St. Mary's Butts.

Another boom for passengers was the ability to board at any point along the route, a situation only possible because conductors were carried. It should also be noted that the Thackrays had a policy of generally employing only mature drivers, whereas conductors generally ranged in age from 16-21. Amongst the earliest drivers were Paddy Cain and Trevor Farrant.

Crews wore dark uniforms in Winter months, with 'winged'hat badges with the letters 'TW' cast into them, whilst for the Summer they were issued with white dust-coats with red lettering on the collars.

NOW IN OPERATION !

NEWBURY'S
NEW LINK TO
LONDON

Via READING, MAIDENHEAD, SLOUGH and COLNBROOK.

THACKRAYS' WAY COACHES

EVERY HOUR DAILY

Single 4/6 Return 6/-

Journey Time : Three Hours.

First Coach Leaves NEWBURY 8.0 a.m.
Last Coach Leaves " 10.0 p.m.

Last Theatre Coach leaves Oxford Circus for Reading 11 30 p.m.

SEE TIME TABLES. Punctuality Always.

MAIN BOOKING OFFICES:
H. MARTIN, Tobacconist, Market Place, Newbury.
C. BREAKSPEAR, 38, West Street, Reading. Phone 2458.
E. W. DURANT, 199, London Road. Phone 719.

31 *Advert from the Newbury Weekly News announcing the Newbury-Reading-London service, which included Gilford coach UV 7966 taken from a photo supplied by the coachbuilder Duple Motors of Hendon.*

 'Thames Valley' responded to the increasing threat by introducing its own 'theatre car', though it only felt demand warranted operation on Wednesdays and Saturdays. However, no enhancement of its daily service was forthcoming at that time.

The Newbury link also directly affected the TV bus service that ran over the same road and had been re-established in 1926. Indeed, Thackray's fare of 1 shilling 9 pence was a penny cheaper for travelling on the luxurious Gilfords than TV charged for a journey that took 10 minutes longer.

It is probable that the TV Board believed that Thackray's investment would not gain the desired rewards, and were therefore willing to wait-and-see. It may also have felt content that there was sufficient traffic on its chosen route to not concern itself with activities along the Bath Road?

However, 'Safeway' did not have such large resources to fall back on, so from November 1929 it switched its service to the route via Wokingham, Bracknell, Ascot and Staines in direct competition with 'Thames Valley'! Timings were revised, with coaches leaving Reading at 9.15am, 1.30pm, 5.30pm and 9.30pm. Return journeys were 11.30am, 3.30pm, 7.30pm and11.30pm. The latter was a 'theatre coach', departing from Charing Cross, and it was possible to book for an outward trip on the 5.30pm at just 2 shillings 6 pence for a night out. The revised schedule evidently only required one coach based in Reading, whilst another probable sign of worsening returns was the offer of cheap day returns at 3 shillings 3 pence after midday on weekdays.

That the 'Thackray's Way' service was well received is acknowledged by the further licence applications made to Reading Borough Council during October 1929. However, this time the application was turned down, thereby commencing a difficult period in relations between the Thackrays and the Borough. Again, road congestion was quoted as the reason for refusal, but Thackray's lodged an appeal with the Minister of Transport. Thackray's had sought licenses for 12 more coaches, 6 of which would also be licensed with Newbury Borough for the Reading to Newbury operation.

As a result of the impending appeal only 6 coaches were ordered for 1929 delivery, duly appearing in November (UW 6646) and December (UW 7597-7601). All were again on Gilford 166SD chassis with Duple dual-doorway 26-seat bodies. It is believed that these were initially used on private hire work, pending the outcome of the licensing appeal.

The delay in expansion was ill-timed, with the approach of the Christmas shopping and pantomime season. However, local coach operator Alf Smith obviously saw it as his opportunity to commence a daily journey to Marble Arch. It is not clear if Smith was testing the water or merely cashing in on the seasonal traffic, but the service was only short-lived.

To make matters worse for 'Thackray's', competition on the road between Slough and London increased with the introduction by 'Highways' of a Windsor–Slough–London service. The latter was of course 'Thackray's' main London agent, so no doubt the process of seeking another agency started as a result of that!

'Thackray's' responded by introducing special fares between Slough and London, but were powerless to introduce the improved frequency it had planned. It should also be noted that there was significant traffic between London and Maidenhead, particularly at weekends, so it is perhaps strange that 'Thames Valley' (which had a large garage in the town) did not act on one of its original proposals to operate a daily service over that route. Much of the traffic was due to Maidenhead having something of a reputation at that time for 'dirty weekends'. Women attracted by the riverside resort, and the men who came there looking for a good time, came down regularly on the coaches, whilst many of the men who had gone there on 'fishing trips' never got their gear out!

Due to the difficulties with the Borough Council in Reading, the Thackrays leased a piece of vacant land adjacent to the Palace Theatre, surrounded by a high wooden fence and bounded by Cheapside, Thorn Street and Friar Street. The site had previously been used by contractors to lay out the special track sections used in the relaying of the West Street tramway junction. Although only rough ground, it did at least give 'Thackray's' an off-road parking ground, which might go some way towards alleviating the Borough's fear of congestion.

With the high mileages being covered by the coaches some mishaps were inevitable. On Thursday 7th November 1929 London-bound Gilford UV 7963 was following a Yorkshire steam lorry on the Bath Road at Taplow.

34 As steam escaped from the lorry the coach driver misjudged his distance, running into the rear of it with some force. Damage to the front end of the coach was extensive and thirteen passengers received injuries. The coach driver, Ernest Grover of Reading, had his hand fractured and was initially trapped by the shattered woodwork of the windscreen.

The aftermath of the brush with a steam wagon near Taplow. Front end damage was quite extensive, but the coach duly returned to service.

As the accident occurred in the busy pre-Christmas period, it has been said that another as yet unlicensed coach (UW 6646?) temporarily assumed the identity of the vehicle under repair!

The appeal to the Minister of Transport was heard on 19th November 1929, but it was a further source of frustration that a decision was delayed until after the Christmas season.

However, Bob Thackray had not been idle during this period, as we shall see next! But, in order to appreciate matters in their full context, we must now return to the events of an earlier period.

35 Chapter Five Pride of the Valley

The Reading area at that time was well served with bus services, either of the 'Thames Valley' or by a myriad of smaller operators running in from the surrounding villages.

Amongst the latter was Harold Cordery, whose 'Pride of the Valley' bus and coach operation was run in conjunction with his garage business. Although 'Thames Valley' (and its predecessor 'British') had already established services between Reading and Shinfield and Reading and Arborfield, Cordery nonetheless commenced his own link between his base at Spencers Wood and Reading. This initially followed the pattern often used by the country carriers in using the yard of a public house as a terminal point. Such action avoided the need to obtain a hackney carriage licence, as the vehicle was not plying for hire on the town's streets. The 'Sun Inn', at the bottom of Castle Street and adjacent to St. Mary's Butts, was chosen for that purpose as it had long been associated with accommodating the carts of the country carriers.

Cordery's initial vehicle was an ex-War Department Crossley 'Tender' chassis, which he had purchased at the Slough Disposal Sales during late 1921. The chassis was fitted with a 14-seater bus body and ran regularly between Spencers Wood and Reading. Precise details of the service are not available, but it is known that some trips were provided for those wishing to attend the cinemas and theatres in Reading. From sometime in 1924 the bus also ran to Basingstoke on Wednesdays and Saturdays to allow market-day shopping in the Hampshire town.

As noted, Harold Cordery had a garage at the main cross-roads in Spencers Wood. Adjacent to that was also the garage business of Harold Healing, who may have had links with Cordery. Whatever the original setup, Healing decided to emigrate to Australia in 1924, selling out to Cordery. The venture was re-titled 'Spencers Wood Garage & Filling Station' and Harold and his family moved into the house behind the former 'Healing's Garage'.

With an enlarged base it was possible to contemplate expansion of his businesses. He took on an additional mechanic named Bob Jackman, of whom we will hear more later on. Probably due to his attention being taken by developments on the garage side and general competition along the Basingstoke Road – including the introduction by 'Thames Valley' of a through Reading–Basingstoke service - Cordery appears to have ceased his regular bus service at this point. However, a Talbot charabanc (MO 7924), with 14-seater body built by Andrews of Newbury, was purchased instead. This saw some use on excursions and probably still operated trips into Reading for the cinema etc.

In the meantime we must back-track a little in time to review the activities of Cecil Rembridge of Ponds End Farm Cottage, in nearby Swallowfield. Mr. Rembridge, in co-operation with William Shadbolt, had commenced a regular bus service from their home village into Reading during the autumn of 1921. Initially they also used an inn yard and avoided the need for hackney carriage licenses. Rembridge registered an Italian-built S.C.A.T. 25hp vehicle as BL 9172 on 30th September 1921. The chassis was actually new in 1913 and is thought to have seen military service in the meantime, coming to Rembridge through Caversham Motors, bearing a black and brown 12-seater 'brake' body.

The service was a success and a second vehicle was placed in service in November 1922, with William Shadbolt then joining him as driver of the S.C.A.T. The two men are believed to have operated a loose partnership, and on 21st November 1922 they placed the route on a more formal footing with Reading Borough Council by obtaining hackney carriage licences for both buses. The additional vehicle was a brown-painted Buick (BL 4472), with 14-seater 'wagonette' body and was purchased from William Vincent of Reading – although it had also seen earlier service as a War Hospital vehicle, being new in 1915.

Rembridge and Shadbolt obtained their licenses to run from Riseley, so that may represent the extension of the original service from Swallowfield. The new Reading terminus was outside Reading Garage Ltd. in Cork Street, just around the corner from St. Mary's Butts.

However, it seems that receipts did not come up to expectations for Bill Shadbolt, and after about six months he went to be a driver for 'Thames Valley' instead! When the licenses came up for renewal on 23rd May 1923 Rembridge renewed that for the Buick only and continued by himself. In

 1924 the established carrier William Platton of Odiham ceased his service through Hook, and Rembridge took the opportunity to extend his route further south to Hook railway station. By that time he had also relocated to Handpost Corner Cottage in Swallowfield. He was joined in January 1924 by his wife Ada, who worked as a conductor at busier times. The S.C.A.T. had not latterly been used much and was withdrawn on 30th September 1924. Its replacement was a new Chevrolet 1-ton (MO 3940), which carried a blue-painted 14-seater bus body and became known locally as ‘Mrs. Hook’.

A second hackney carriage license was obtained from Reading Borough and that was in connection with further route developments. Rembridge evidently did not trouble the Borough with too much detail over how he was adding to the places served beyond its boundaries. Some journeys to Heckfield were added, presumably as a result of the cessation of a similar service by Sunner Lovegrove of Silchester. This is apparently confirmed by the appearance of Herb Nash, who had been the driver of Lovegrove’s bus, and it is believed that he injected some money into the expansion of Rembridge’s operations.

Further variant routes were developed, all from Reading, to reach Beech Hill, Farley Hill and the Wellington Monument – the latter point being very popular for picnics and rambles on Heckfield Heath. Precise dates are not known, but all were in place by April 1926, at which point Rembridge had again relocated to Farley Hill. These links proved very popular locally and a further Chevrolet 1-ton (MO 7526), also with blue-painted 14-seater bus body, was placed in service on 7th April 1926.

Whether or not Rembridge had over-stretched his finances is not certain but, in December 1926, he evidently disposed of his newer Chevrolet and his right to the licence on the Reading – Hook service to Harold Cordery. The licence was formally transferred to him on 21st December, but Rembridge continued his other services

It should be noted that ‘Thames Valley’ had in fact recently improved its operations along the Basingstoke Road with new Tilling-Stevens saloons. The company was also generally referred to locally as ‘the Valley’, so it perhaps no mere coincidence that Cordery choose the title ‘Pride of the Valley’ for his return to bus operation? In fact the valley referred to in his case was that of the River Loddon, but one still senses some mischief in the choice, particularly as he also adopted a similar red and white livery as well!

It soon became evident that a larger vehicle was required, and just before Christmas 1926 he was able to obtain a new off-the-peg Thornycroft from their Basingstoke works. Registered MO 9039, it was an A1-type with Vickers 20-seater bus body. The Thornycroft took over the main route from the first day of 1927, whilst the Chevrolet provided short-workings to the other villages previously served by Rembridge.

Harold Cordery's first Thornycroft bus was this neat 20-seater MO 9039.

Cordery decided to seek a license for the service to Heckfield, which of course Rembridge had not held, but on 22nd March 1927 he found his application deferred until he could provide the Chief Constable with a timetable. This requirement was duly met and the license granted from 19th April, though the terminus had to be moved to Blagrave Street as part of the Borough's policy of pushing standing buses out from the main roads in the town.

This policy duly resulted in 'Thames Valley' being ordered to quit St. Mary's Butts, despite the use of that terminus since it arrived in July 1915!

39 The earlier contact with Thornycrofts resulted in the opportunity to purchase several former demonstration vehicles, the first of which arrived in May 1927. Registered HO 6335 in September 1924, it was a much larger 'Boadicea' type, with very upright dual-doorway 26-seat bus body by Vickers. It had been with Devon Motor Transport at one point, but the gear change was difficult to master and the bus was a 'pig' to hand-start!

The second Thornycroft was HO 6335, seen here when in use as a demonstrator for its Basingstoke-based makers.

Private hire work was also pursued more vigorously as further drivers were employed and vehicles of varied capacities could be offered.

As a further development of services, some journeys on certain days on the Reading – Hook route were diverted to serve Mattingley Green.

The 'Pride of the Valley' buses were popular, as they were able to respond better to local needs, such as the 11.00pm departure from Reading. So much so, that in September 1927 Harold Cordery sought to further expand his operations. He applied to Reading Borough for two licenses, one for a bus between Reading and Arborfield via Shinfield, and another from Reading northwards to Peppard Sanatorium. However, both were refused on the grounds that the roads were already adequately served by others.

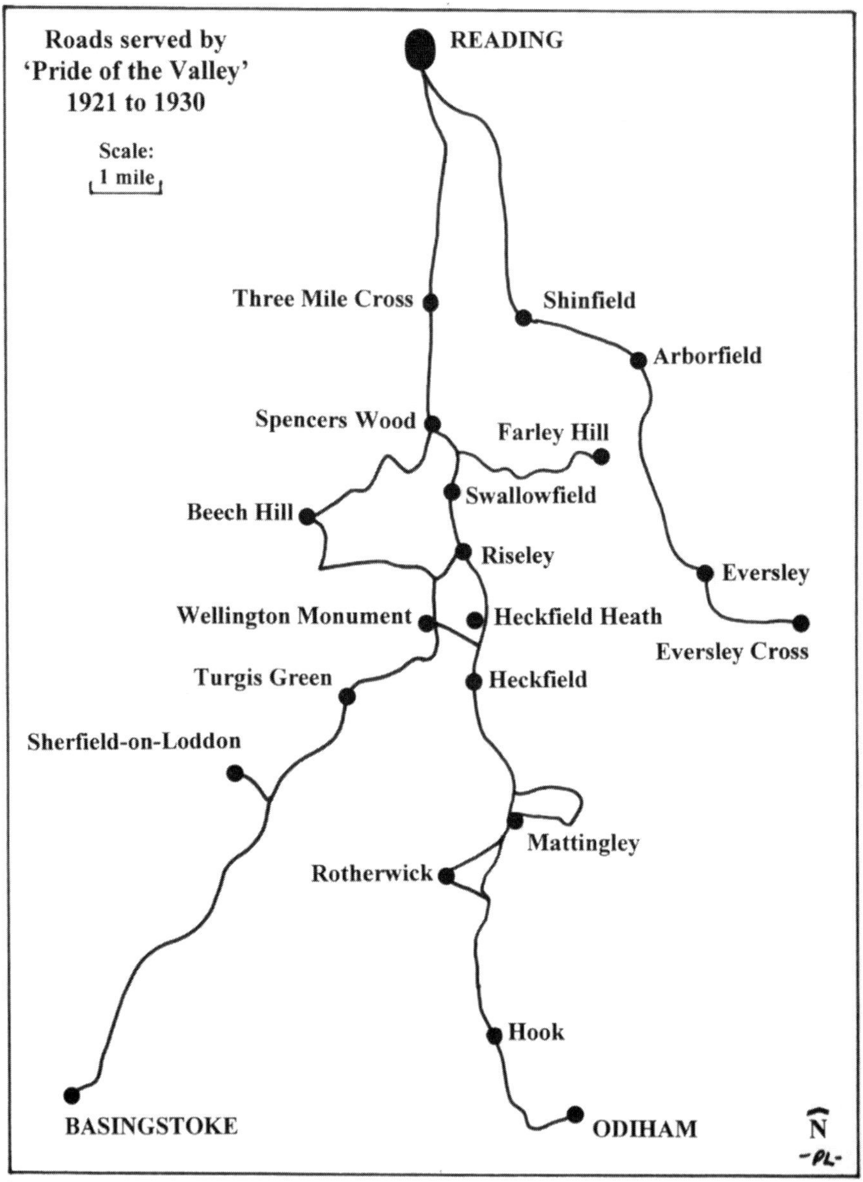

This map indicates the fullest extent of services operated by Harold Cordery's 'Pride of the Valley' fleet.

41 The second former Thornycroft demonstrator arrived in November 1927 in the shape of OT 1339. New in May 1926 it was a LB-type with a very sleak 30-seater rear-entrance bus body. Local man Ted Baylis, who it is believed had previously driven for Rembridge, joined at about this time and is believed to have contributed to the purchase of this vehicle. He became its regular driver, and it was also used on private hire as it was a comfortable vehicle. However, it is recalled for disgracing itself in Southampton Street on one occasion, shedding two wheels which went through a shop window! Apparently work on it had not been completed when it was taken from the garage, the wheels having not been fully tightened.

The second former Thornycroft demonstrator to be acquired was OT 1339, an LB-type with a sleak body by Hall Lewis.

Cordery met Rembridge in early 1928 and made an offer for his remaining operations. This was accepted, but it must be appreciated that the latter held no licenses for them, as he had continued to run them from the 'Sun Inn'. Cordery sought to remedy this situation, but found himself in the middle of a row over the number of buses operating out of Reading along the Basingstoke Road!

The Borough Council instructed the Chief Constable to take a survey of such journeys, deferring any decisions relating to that road until the May meeting. At the same time the Borough found itself the recipient of representations from Arborfield Parish Council and Wokingham Rural District Council, each wanting to see better services at lower fares.

Rembridge's Chevrolet (MO 3940) was acquired, but laid up unused by the garage. Instead two Chevrolet LM-types were ordered whilst the license applications were being sorted out. The first was registered on 8th February 1928 as RX 1590 and fitted with a 14-seater body intended for use on some of the very narrow roads locally. The other Chevrolet duly appeared on 2nd March 1928 as RX 1456, having been fitted with a third axle and a 20-seater bus body. Such chassis conversions enjoyed some popularity at that time, as the investment of under £100 gave 50% more seats.

During the early months of 1928 Cordery continued to operate the buses on the ex-Rembridge services out of the 'Sun Inn' yard. Despite the expression of encouragement he had previously received from the WRDC, he found himself on the receiving end in May when it wrote complaining that his bus was breaking up the road surfaces the Farley Hill area. The following month a complaint had been received regarding the speed of his buses over the same road!

The three Thornycrofts are believed to have continued to cover the routes for which licences were held during this period. When the Reading Borough Council's Hackney Carriage Sub-committee met on 22nd May, it refused Cordery's additional licenses.

Harold Cordery reacted to this by withdrawing the through services to Farley Hill and Beech, instead substituting 'feeder' connections that met the buses on the main route outside the 'George & Dragon'at Three Mile Cross. This avoided the need to have a permission from Reading Borough, whilst only presenting the passengers with minimal inconvenience.

Beech Hill was served by diverting the Reading–Sherfield-on-Loddon buses between Spencers Wood and Heckfield Common, which was out of the Borough Council's area. Farley Hill had a feeder service, almost always worked by the 6-wheel Chevrolet and driven by Abey Lailey.

Other staff evident at this point were 'Pod' Norris and Len Towner (both conductors), and drivers Fred Tigwell and Fred Doddington (regular with

43 the Thornycroft A1), together with apprentice fitters Maurice ('Nobby') Earley and Tom Lake.

Young Maurice Earley (left), with Bill Jackman on motorbike and and brother Joe Earley.

It should be noted that Maurice Earley's father was James George Earley of Spencers Wood, who had in fact provided some passenger-carrying facilities locally using his International lorry (BL 9299). Although generally used for haulage and coal delivery, it could be fitted with 14 seats to transport sports teams or dance parties, some seaside excursions and regular cinema/theatre trips to Reading on a Saturday evening. Indeed, 'Nobby' recalls that one year his father took £92 in fares – which was more than he made from haulage work!

James had paid £48 to Harold Cordery for his 14-year old son to undertake a three-year motor engineering apprenticeship commencing on 1st January 1928. Although that was not specifically related to Cordery's buses, right from the beginning 'Nobby' took a particular interest in them. On Saturdays he would sometimes act as conductor on the Reading-Hook service, even getting a chance to try his hand behind the wheel if he was lucky. On occasions the bus became so full, he would ride on it wedged between the front mudguard and the bonnet! Indeed, we shall hear more of his career in due course.

The ongoing attitude of Reading Borough Council meant that Cordery had difficulty in obtaining further licenses for buses operating into the town, so 1928 largely saw him consolidating his existing operations. However, all was perhaps not entirely well, as he approached 'Thames Valley' in October of that year to see if it wished to buy him out. TV considered his asking price of £3,500 too high and told him so. In the end that action would cost the company dearly indeed!

By 1st April 1929 he had extended his Heckfield route onwards, via the 'Earl Derby' and North Warnborough, to Odiham.

Not that he had completely given up with the Borough, as he applied for a bus to be used on a Reading–Arborfield–Eversley service, which was already running in response to appeals he had received from Arborfield Parish Council. The Parish Council wrote to Reading Borough in support of the application, explaining that the first departure by 'Thames Valley' precluded being able to reach Reading before 11.00am. Although TV did respond with an earlier service, the Parish Council was still of the opinion that Cordery's small bus was more suitable and more appropriately timed.

The licence in respect of that route was not granted when a decision was made on 23rd July 1929, though the Borough Council did allow one more licence for a vehicle to be used on the existing services, thereby defeating any desire to restrict the number of buses entering the town! As it was, Cordery continued with the Eversley service, resorting again to the use of the 'Sun Inn' yard for the unlicensed bus.

Also on the very same day, and in apparent contradiction of its avowed policy, the Borough also granted a licence to F.J. Lintott of Basingstoke for a bus on a Reading–Basingstoke route!

Talbot chara MO7924 is seen with a party heading for an historical pageant in Reading Abbey ruins.

The Talbot charabanc (MO 7924) had remained in service, latterly repainted in red, but was laid up at the end of September 1929. In the normal course of events, it would have returned to use the following spring. At about the same time the ex-Rembridge Chevrolet (MO 7526) was also withdrawn for the winter. The Thornycroft A1 was repainted red and cream (from red and white) to match the newer Chevrolets.

Harold Cordery was however troubled by increased competition along the Basingstoke Road. Not only had 'Thames Valley' steadily improved its timings, but had recently introduced Leyland 'Titan' double-deckers on that route. Added to that, Mr. Lintott's small initial incursion had grown from

8th October 1929 to include a Reading-Odiham service under the title 'Direct Bus Service'.

The whole situation had caused Reading Borough Council to decide that it would in future reduce the daily coverage on that road from 150 to 103 journeys. The irony of the situation was that it was the Council's own inconsistent decisions that had largely created the situation. And certainly it seemed unmoved by both the requirements of those who lived in the surrounding villages and the pleas of the traders who wanted to see more people attracted to the town to offset the trade depression then being felt!

The frustrations experienced by both Harold Cordery and Bob Thackray led to the two operators holding discussions during November 1929. It is not entirely clear if Thackray had intended to continue the routes south of Reading on a long-term basis. However, the acquisition of existing licenses proved itself valuable, as will also be noted in due course.

Transfer of 'Pride of the Valley' took place around 1st December 1929, with the Borough Council allowing transfer of the six licenses on the 17th of that month. The buses continued to be garaged at Cordery's premises, and arrangements were made for Bob Jackman, the senior mechanic, to take care of their maintenance.

Young 'Nobby', by then approaching the final year of his apprenticeship (and earning 15 shillings per week) was also keen to stay involved with the buses. He therefore spoke to Harold Cordery, who was willing to release him if Thackray's would employ him. The latter had somewhat worn its welcome out at the Vincent's Station Hill site and, towards the end of 1929, had taken a short-term lease on Vincent's old premises in Castle Street, where minor maintenance was more practical and coaches could be washed and refuelled. Ernest Cory, the Depot Manager, interviewed 'Nobby' and took him on for the night shift 8.30pm – 8.30am, six days a week for £1. He did running repairs and lubrication and some shunting of coaches. Fortunately he had his own motorcycle by then, so he was free to travel to and from work as needed.

So, the Thackrays once again found themselves as bus operators in addition to the express coaches and taxicabs.

Chapter Six A Masterstroke

Soon after the acquisition of 'Pride of the Valley' the decision was taken to overhaul the three Thornycrofts (HO 6335, OT 1339 and MO 9039), and the two Chevrolets (RX 1456 and RX 1590) for continued service.

The Thornycrofts were dealt with first, being taken to the London workshops in Ledbury Mews West, before returning in a new livery of dark red and cream. Whilst they were absent their place was taken by Gilford coaches, but all returned to Spencers Wood. The Chevrolets also went for overhaul in London, but they did not return to their former base. The withdrawn Chevrolet (MO 7526) and the Talbot chara (MO 7924) were disposed off. This had the effect of leaving Thackrays with one unused license, which they wisely retained for possible later re-allocation.

A further batch of Gilford coaches, with similar Duple bodies, had been received during January and February 1930, with some covering for the Thornycrofts away for attention. The full batch was GC 1866-1871, all of the 2 inches longer 168SD type, with a more powerful 6 litre Lycoming engine, and those not yet in service were stored at the back of the Spencers Wood garage pending the approval of further licenses.

Returning to developments on 'Thackray's Way' services, the Reading terminus and interchange point for the Reading–Maidenhead–London and Reading–Newbury services was transferred to the Palace Theatre parking ground by January 1930.

Former Cordery employee Fred Doddington, who lived in St. Mary's Butts between 'The Horn' and Hosier Street, was taken on to act as the Traffic Superintendent at that location. At other times he would go out on the road to check on punctuality and look out for conductors on the fiddle, one of his favourite spots being the stop at 'The Bear' in Maidenhead. His area covered Newbury to Maidenhead, whilst his London-based colleague Pennington looked after the section between London and Maidenhead. Fred was a well-known local character and was somewhat cross-eyed. He left Reading to work in Twickenham for about a year from early 1936, but then returned to Reading as the licensee of 'The Britannia Tap' in Caversham Road.

 However, the Thackrays once again found themselves faced with a refusal by the Borough Council to issue further licenses for coaches on the London and Newbury services. Again, it was the pressure of such traffic that concerned the authority, particularly as the number of through coaches using Reading as a 'convenience stop' had increased over the preceding couple of years.

Thackrays once again appealed to the Minister of Transport, but found that he upheld the refusal when the decision was made in mid-January. Bob was, however, not to be beaten by this hardening of attitude on the part of the Council, and he sought an urgent meeting with the Hackney Carriage Sub-committee to discuss the situation.

He had of course already done his homework before the meeting, taking the Councillors completely by surprise with his bold proposal! Thackray offered to construct a purpose-built coaching station adjacent to Cemetery Junction, the point at which the two main east-west routes to London met. The site would become the home for the 'Thackray's Way' fleet, whilst also providing extensive refreshment and toilet facilities for through coaches.

Thus, in one masterstoke, Bob was able turn the fortunes of the Reading-based operations around yet again!

That the Council was indeed very happy with the proposal is evidenced by the granting on 21st January 1930 of twelve further licences, six each for the Newbury and London services.

During the latter part of January 1930 the London service was improved to a 40-minute headway, with departures from 7.00am through to 11.00pm. Return journeys commenced at 7.30am, followed by 8.30am by way of the coaches stabled overnight in London, before going onto the 40 minute pattern until the 'theatre coach' at 11.30pm. The revised times only applied to Monday-Saturdays operations, whereas Sundays were served by the previous hourly pattern.

On the Reading–Newbury service the frequency was increased from 40 minutes to 30 minutes, with the first coach leaving Reading at 7.00am and returning from Newbury at 8.00am. Coaches continued to run on that route

49 until the last return journey left Newbury at 11.00pm. On Sundays the frequency was maintained, though the service started two journeys later in the day.

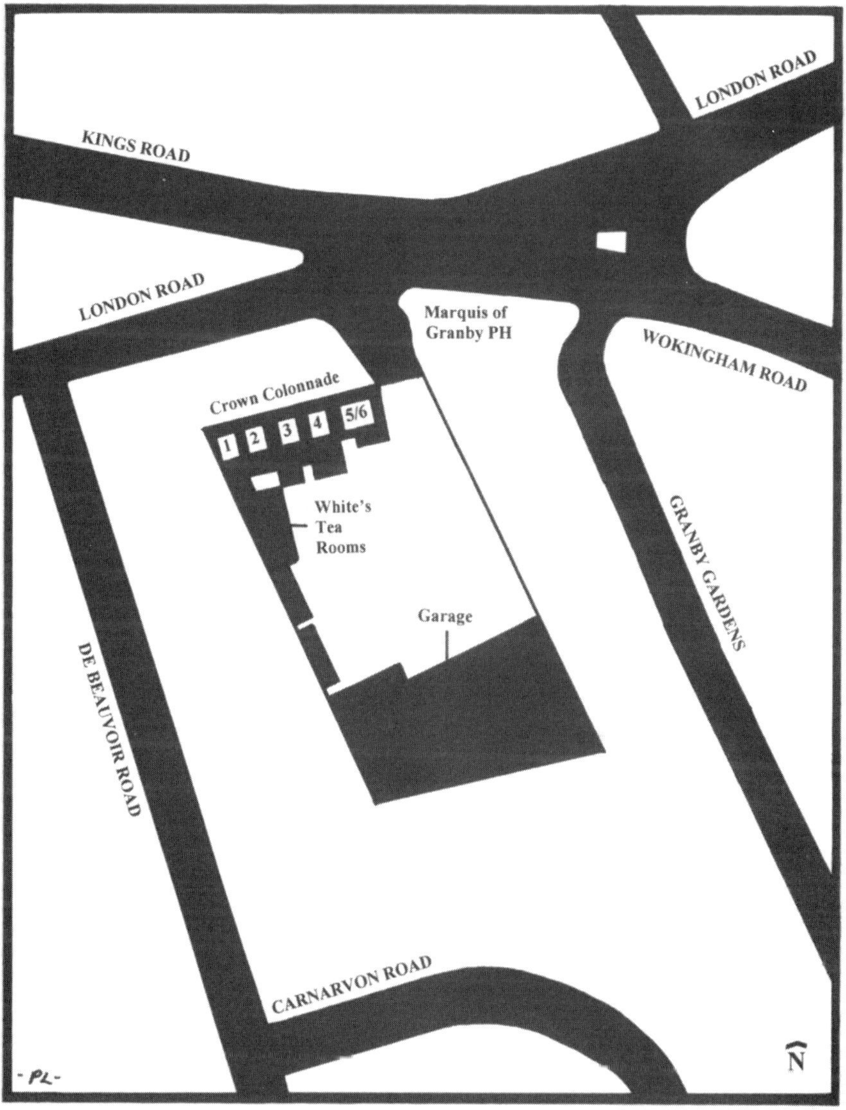

THE CROWN COLONNADE
AND COACHING STATION

However, with the commitment to cover for absent ex-Cordery vehicles, it was soon found difficult to maintain the new schedules. Some adjustments were therefore made with effect from 12th February 1930. By re-timing the London service to a 45-minute headway it proved possible to reduce the number of weekday daily return journeys from 24 to 22. However, the Newbury service did benefit from some improvements at the same time. An earlier 6.30am departure from Reading was introduced, which formed the 7.30am return trip. The last departure from Reading on weekdays was an additional 10.30pm trip, returning from Newbury as the 11.30pm. On Saturdays only these were further enhanced by the addition of an 11.00pm departure from Reading which returned from Newbury at midnight. All of these amendments had the dual effect of generating more local passengers, in respect of pleasure traffic, whilst improving the feeder opportunities to/from the London service.

The new timetable for February also saw the appearance of a rhyme based on the company's operating name:

'Thackray's Way'

The service that picks you up, but never lets you down.

Travel in comfort by modern saloon
Half-hourly service provides a real boon*
Always convenient for visits to town
Calling en route to pick up and set down
Kindly ask driver for booklet and see
Reading and London connected by me
At your service for shopping, business or pleasure
You just board a coach and go at your leisure
Swiftly and safely by super saloon

Wafted as smoothly as in a balloon
And after your first trip I venture to say
Your Way will always be Thackray's Way

(Thackray's had hoped to introduce a 30-minute headway by that time)*

51 On 18th February 1930 Reading Borough granted Thackrays an additional licence for the Reading–Maidenhead–London service in place of the unused one held over from the ex-Cordery Talbot charabanc that had been disposed of.

Again, though not everything went the right way for the Thackrays as, no sooner than they had improved the London service, they found a new competitor running between Windsor, Slough and London from 27th January. This was yet another London 'pirate' operator that had turned to express coaches and ran under the name 'Premier Omnibus Co.'.

As will be recalled, Thackray's had been using the London booking agent 'Highways Ltd.', but the latter's decision to enter the field as an operator caused them to seek alternative arrangements. A joint booking office was set up with another operator (not in competition over their routes) in the shape of 'Skylark', another London-based firm with both a taxicab business and a fleet of Gilford coaches. The office was at 288 Regent Street, virtually across the road from 'Highways', with the new arrangement coming into place from early February 1930.

The effects of the improved 'Thackray's Way' services did however start to show on the competition during early 1930. 'Thames Valley' withdrew its 'theatre coach' facility and altered the timings in order to base both vehicles for the route at Reading. 'Safeway' again revamped its timings, but that would not prove to be its salvation, as will be duly noted.

'Thames Valley' had certainly under-estimated the newcomer, and it soon became clear that it must address the situation urgently. In respect of the Reading-Newbury service, an additional vehicle was sent to Newbury shed, allowing for an increase in headway from 45 to 30 minutes from 15th March 1930.

About March 1930 work got underway on the new coaching station near Cemetery Junction. The site was formerly the Crown Nursery of Messrs Wilson & Agar and, as the site was relatively clear to start with progress was quite rapid, with three large petrol tanks with a capacity of 15,000 gallons arriving for installation beneath the yard surface in April 1930. It is of course interesting to note that both the London and Reading garages were connected with former nursery sites.

52 The site covered a large area fronting northwards onto London Road, and bounded to the east by Granby Gardens and to the west by De Beauvoir Road. Some of the cottages abutting the site in Granby Gardens were also acquired at some point. Work on the garage was substantially complete by June, when it become operational.

Somewhat surprisingly no photos of the coach station in its original form have come to light. However, this 1950's view shows the large 2-bay shed constructed to house the coach fleet. The petrol pumps remain in situ on their island, but are no longer for public use. The shed to the right was a later addition by 'Thames Valley' to allow body overhauls on double-decks.

At the rear of the site was constructed a large steel-framed garage capable of housing all of the fleet and more, together with an area for overhauls and bodywork/painting. It should be appreciated that all major overhauls had, until then, been undertaken at Ledbury Mews. The large yard area included a petrol-filling island to the eastern boundary, fitted with the latest type of air-operated pumps dispensing 'Power' petrol. A coach and motor servicing facility was offered from the start, together with a 24-hour breakdown service. The company also became the local Gilford spares stockist.

Further forward and against the western boundary was a large wooden building that opened slightly later as the passenger restaurant. Unlike the other facilities, that were run by Thackray's directly, it was contracted out to Messrs White & Stevens. It duly became known as 'White's Tea Rooms', as Kathleen Stevens had married Arthur White within a year, and it was open all day to satisfy the needs of coach passengers. According to 'Thackray's Way' letterheads of the period, the restaurant could accommodate 150 persons, whilst the yard had room for 100 coaches (though the latter was actually amended to 100 cars instead).

Indeed, most if not all the through coach operators switched their 'comfort stop' to the new location once it was available, with 'Thackray's' also becoming their booking agent on the east of Reading.

Behind this selection of normal-control Gilford coaches are the stairs and walkway serving the flats above the Crown Colonnade shops. To the left is part of the extensive refreshment and rest-rooms complex. Coaches shown are (left to right) GC 1867, GJ 1331, GJ 1332 and GC 1871 of 1929 - 1930.

At the front of the site, and obscuring all of the above from the gaze of passers-by, was the Crown Colonnade, named in perpetuation of the former nursery, a parade of four shops with flats over which were rented out. To the east of the parade, but built as a separate unit known as 5/6 Crown Colonnade, was office accommodation and an enquiry and booking office which became the new registered office for the 'Ledbury Transport Co. Ltd.'. At that point Bob's son Frederick Robert Thackray also became a director.

The original tenants of the Crown Colonnade shop premises were:
No.1 White & Stevens (The Colonnade Café); No.2 Miss D. H. Green, Ladies Hairdresser; No.3 William Arthur, Tailor; No.4 W. E. Harwood Ltd., Bootmakers

A 1950's view of the Crown Colonnade. The shops were numbered 1 to 6 from right to left. Note the 'Thames Valley' booking office opened post-war.

In addition to the above businesses, the flats above each unit were let out, and that above 5/6 housed the Depot Manager Ernest Cory (who had transferred from London) and his wife Alice. Electricity to the garage complex was generated on site using a Platt stationery engine.

Yet another competitor raised its head on the Windsor-Slough-London road, when the 'London General' commenced a 30-minute headway from 20th April 1930 – with the added attraction of through fares to some Underground stations.

However, again we must back-track a little in order to cover other important events that shaped the future of 'Thackray's Way'.

Whilst construction of the depot was under way the company suffered an unexpected set back to its plans on the night of Thursday 30th April 1930.

The Spencers Wood buses had come off service during the evening and been refuelled before being backed into the garage. The Night Foreman Bob Jackman was there finishing up his duties about 3.45am when he noticed petrol leaking onto the floor from the Thornycroft A1 (MO 9039). As it was a cold night there was a coke brazier alight to keep the buses warm enough for starting in the morning – a recipe for disaster under the circumstances!

Bob attempted to tighten the thread of the fuel pipe which was leaking, not realising that a fracture had occurred, resulting in about 14 gallons of petrol gushing out across the floor and being ignited by the brazier. Despite the efforts of the three cleaners also on duty in using fire extinguishers, the fire soon spread.

All that remained of the Thornycroft MO 9039 and the 3 new Gilford coaches after the Spencers Wood fire was this tangled mass of scrap.

 Eight vehicles were in and around the garage, one parked by the garage wall and two further away. Quickly Bob drove out a Gilford coach that formed the front of the line up, but the spreading fire prevented him removing further vehicles from inside. He did, however, manage to move the Thornycroft BX (HO 6335) away from the garage wall shortly before it collapsed– the bus starting first time for once!

Bob Jackman poses by the fire-scorched Thornycroft OT 1339.

The Wokingham Fire Brigade were soon on the scene and stopped the fire reaching an underground fuel tank, but the A1 was lost, together with three almost new Gilfords (GC 1866/8/9), whilst the garage was completely destroyed. The remains of the three Gilford chassis were towed to Bob Thackray's farm at Calcot, where any useful parts were salvaged. In all some £7000 worth of damage was caused, though most was covered by insurance.

There are two amusing asides to this otherwise serious event. The first concerns 'Nobby's' visit to the site to see what could be salvaged when, sifting through the debris, he was able to pick up some of the change that had survived from the conductor's bags. The other centres on the local police constable PC Harvey, who was actually on the premises having an (unofficial) cup of tea. Although he raised the alarm whilst Bob moved the buses, he still had to explain why he had lost his helmet which had fallen victim to the fire!

Both Bob Jackman and cleaner Charlie Sheady were both slightly burned, but there is no doubt that the staff's prompt action reduced the potential losses.

No blame was attached to Bob Jackman, who continued to work for Thackrays. After a while he transferred to the London depot, but soon got a job collecting Beardmore taxis from their Paisley works for cab operators in London. Later he returned to Reading as Works Manager with Great Western Motors Ltd.

As a consequence of the Spencers Wood fire, the company found itself with an accommodation problem, but Vincents again helped out by permitting the buses for those services to be kept in the yard its Station Hill site pending completion of the new garage.

Three replacement licences were granted in lieu of the 'vehicles lost in the Spencers Wood fire'. In reality that description was not strictly accurate, as not all the Gilfords had had the benefit of RBC licences, whereas the Chevrolets had survived by virtue of being away in London at the time! There is little doubt that this was a case of slightly bending the facts in order to increase the fleet strength

As the completion of the coaching station neared 'Thackray's' once again approached the Borough Council regarding the granting of further licenses in time for consideration on 20th May 1930. In view of the evidence that Bob Thackray had indeed kept his side of the bargain, the Council was in a more conciliatory frame of mind, resulting in six more licences being awarded for the Reading–Maidenhead–London route.

The additional licenses at last gave 'Thackray's Way' the opportunity to institute an improved service on the London route from 4th June 1930. The new pattern gave a 30-minute headway from 6.30am through to 11.00pm on weekday departures from Reading, with the coaches diverting via the new coaching station. At this time the scheduled running time was increased from 2 hours to 2 hours and 12 minutes. The terminal point remained the parking ground of the Palace Theatre, where the Newbury service continued to run from. The latter service did, however, lose its late-night return journey between Reading and Newbury.

The revised scheduled called for ten coaches, three of which were based at Ledbury Mews and exchanged on a daily rotation, whilst six crews worked out of the London premises. Additional Gilford 168SD coaches with similar Duple bodies were added during April 1930 (GF 6676-9), in May (GJ 1331/2) and in June (GJ 8024). The last three were the insurance replacements for the three 'GC' registered coaches lost in the fire. Apparently the Thornycroft A1 had not actually been insured at that time.

As already noted, there is little doubt that 'Safeway' ceased as a result of improved operations by both 'Thackray's' and 'Thames Valley'. Indeed, the latter had already planned an improved timetable, which came into effect on Friday 16th May 1930. Ten daily journeys were operated, starting from Reading at 7.30am and with headway that varied from one hour to 90 minutes until the last departure at 7.30pm. All journeys returned to Reading, with the last departure at 10.00pm. TV had already been forced to reduce the adult return fare from 6 shillings to 4 shillings in order to match 'Safeway' from Wednesday 1st January 1930, and that fare remained in place.

In order to cover the new schedules, and perhaps to convince the more sceptical directors of its worth, temporary arrangements were made to cover the service. Tilling-Stevens 159 and 160 remained on the route, but were joined by Leyland 'Lion' LT1-type saloons from the Brush bus-bodied 209-218 (RX 5571-80) batch, which had been delivered during January and

 February 1930. The latter were duly replaced from July 1930 with the delivery of 'Lion' LT2-types 225-9 (RX 6245-49), with semi-luxury bodies. Joining them was a 6-cylinder-engined Leyland 'Tiger' TS3, car 230 (RX 6250), which carried a very luxurious coach body by Brush, and had been ordered to assess the type's performance on the route.

A major step forward in the 'Thames Valley' battle with 'Thackray's Way' was the purchase of this Leyland Tiger TS3 with 29-seater coach body by Brush Coachworks of Loughborough. A Lion-type radiator was fitted in order to allow a 'Thames Valley' radiator badge to be accommodated on the top tank.

Again, it would appear that TV was content to return to sole operation on the Reading–Ascot–London route, without resorting to challenging 'Thackray's' on the route via Maidenhead – despite the existence of a large depot in that town and membership of London Coastal Coaches. Even the established TV service between Reading and Newbury, which was worked from both ends, saw no significant improvements as 'Thackray's' stole traffic away through faster operations and more comfortable rolling stock.

However, some more short-lived competition between London (Charing Cross) and Maidenhead appeared during May 1930, when 'Pring's Motor Coach Service' of London tried to tap into the 'pleasure traffic' with five journeys a day.

 'Premier' also increased the frequency on its Windsor–Slough-London service to a 15-minute headway from 12th June 1930.

'Premier' also ran Leyland Tiger TS3 coaches, including GN 5150 shown above in Slough High Street whilst working the Windsor – Slough – London service. This carried a 26-seater body by London Lorries of Kentish Town and was new in 1931. It later passed with two similar coaches to 'Thames Valley', who also ran it through Slough to London for a time.

The Thackrays were never content with the status quo, and a re-assessment of their plans inevitably followed the Spencers Wood fire.

With the new garage and coaching station up and running and rents from the restaurant, shop premises and flats, together with income from tolls levied on visiting coaches, further expansion could at last be considered. There were risks involved, of course, and it is believed that some (if not all) of the coaches were originally obtained on hire-purchase agreements. Indeed, it has been said that Bob's wife Alice often fretted that he would over-stretch himself as the coach business expanded, and she provided a restraining influence at times.

However, it is necessary to return to other events of the Spring of 1930 in order to fully appreciate the overall scenario about to unfold.

61 Chapter Eight Chequebook Diplomacy

Whilst the coaching station was under construction Bob Thackray had also been busy talking to some other local coach operators with a view to purchasing their businesses.

Quite who instigated the negotiations is unclear, but the general economic climate was deteriorating, and Reading's traditional trades were being badly affected. Understandably, certain of the local coach operators who relied on income from excursion work were eyeing the coming season with some concern.

It was against that background that Bob found several operators willing to accept his offer. His real motive however, was not so much to acquire more excursion work, but he was more interested in acquiring the hackney licences attached to their vehicles!

Three concerns were acquired, but others may have been approached at the same time. The first to sell was Albert E. Ireland, proprietor of the 'Alexandra Coaches', a business that had seen something of a rise and fall in its six years of existence.

Bert had originally driven a charabanc for Charlie Tanton (who we will hear more of in due course) in 1922, passing with him in 1923 into the partnership of 'Tanton & Smith'. He evidently decided to try his own hand at chara work in 1924, and is also believed to have commenced a garage business at the same time. The impetus was of course the very busy excursions trade caused by the staging of the British Empire Exhibition at Wembley in 1924/5.

The garage was situated at the junction of London Road and Alexandra Road, the name 'Alexandra' being adopted for both the chara and the garage. Very soon he was advertising a choice of 14, 18, 20 and 28-seaters for hire, although research shows that these cannot have all been in his ownership. A likely explanation is that he kept on good terms with his old boss Charlie Tanton, who had an acrimonious split with Alf Smith in early 1924, with Ireland hiring additional coaches from him as required.

The only chara known to have been owned was an American-built GMC that had apparently been one of a number savaged from a ship that had sunk in a British river estuary. Its identity is not known, though it was not registered locally. This 20-seater continued in use at the time that he sold out to the Thackrays.

The garage business had already been disposed of, so part of the deal was that Bert would be employed by 'Thackray's Way', and he became a driver for a short time. However he 'disappeared' for while from the local scene, but was driving for 'Smith's Coaches' at the outbreak of the Second World War, before a spell with 'Thames Valley'. After the war he returned to Smith's, but on the hire cars, before moving to London to become a taxi driver. He was a bit of a 'character' and always wore a bow-tie.

However, Bob Thackray must have got a shock when the Council initially deferred, and then rejected, his application to transfer the license on the GMC to him in May 1930. Not to be outdone, he had the charabanc body removed, before the vehicle took up a new role as a breakdown tender at the Colonnade Garage!

The only known photo of Gilford RD 1886 with its original 'allweather' body acquired with the business of Charlie Tanton of Reading.

63 The acquisition of Charlie Tanton's coach business based in Orts Road may have had a connection with Ireland's decision to sell, in view of the two operator's previous co-operation. There had been a proposal for a number of the local operators to combine as 'BBB Coaches', but that had not materialised. Once again, the prevailing economic climate was doubtless the reason for acceptance of the offer, and employment with the new owners was part of the deal.

A recent modernisation had taken place with the addition of two Gilford coaches in 1929/30. One was a forward-control 168OT-type (RD 1886), which carried a 30-seater dual-doorway 'allweather' body with a canvas roof throughout the central section. This layout actually proved to be the vehicle's undoing in the end, as there was not enough strength in the remaining framework, interrupted by two doorways and a large open section of roof! It is even a possibility that the body was one of the short-lived fashion for canvas-covered bodies, which were lightweight but prone to damage!

Former Tanton Gilford VM 8638 was also acquired during 1930.

 The second Gilford coach was of the normal-control 166SD-type (VM 8638), new in 1929 and evidently originally with a Manchester-based operator. RD had the Gruss air suspension system, whereas VM did not.

Indeed, Tanton may have been regretting further investment in the business after the 1929 Wall Street Crash, and the offer from Thackray may have come at a good time?

Two of E.M. Hope's Vincent-bodied charabancs, Delahaye DP 7669 and Dennis DP 3590, on an outing in July 1928.

Another operator in Reading found to be willing to sell out was Edward Molesworth Hope, whose Vincent-bodied 20-seater Dennis charabanc (DP 3590) took to the road at the end of March 1921. His base was 154 Castle Hill, and for the 1926 season he added an Italian-built Lancia 20-seater (DP 3???), followed by another 20-seater in June of that year. The latter also had a body by Vincent of Reading, but was on a Delahaye chassis built in France and registered DP 7669.

The trio of vehicles passed to Thackrays in June 1930, making a total of six hackney carriage licences for future transfer to new replacement coaches in the 'Thackray's Way' fleet. But, before they could be replaced, each vehicle would give service of one kind or another to its new owners, as will be noted in due course.

Chapter Nine Of Men and Machines

So far we have followed the progress of the development of 'Thackray's Way'. However despite the undeniable energy of the Thackray family in bringing this to fruition, it could have only been achieved through the efforts of their workforce. Also of particular relevance to the success of the enterprise was the choice of rolling stock, and in this chapter we will explore both of these important aspects.

Apart from the motley collection of buses and coaches purchased in local take-overs, none of which was kept any longer than dictated by pure necessity, the choice fell to the use of Gilford chassis.

One of the original batch of Duple-bodied Gilford coaches, UV 7964 stops at The Bear Hotel in Maidenhead. Also note the adjacent booking office for coach services, including those affiliated to London Coastal Coaches.

The Gilford Motor Co.Ltd., originally based in the Holloway Road, London N7, but at a new factory in High Wycombe from 1927, was unusual in that it manufactured hardly any of the parts utilised in its chassis. What they did was to assemble together the best available engines, gearboxes, axles and suspension systems, many of the engines being Lycoming units from

 America. In doing so they produced a modern, fast chassis at a price affordable by the mushrooming array of independent operators. All but the initial batch with UV registrations were fitted with Gruss air suspension, which worked by means of cylinders positioned at the front end of the chassis frame on each side of the radiator.

Even the chassis designation had an American flavour, with the suffix 'SD' standing for 'standard drive' and 'OT' for 'overtype', in place of the more familiar 'normal-control' and 'forward-control' used in Britain.

The maintenance staff also recall the Gilfords very favourably, as they were relatively easy to maintain, whilst the drivers appreciated the powerful engines and efficient four-wheel brakes. The only criticism was the tendency for the radiator to boil, but that could be remedied.

Upon these chassis were placed very high standard bodies, incorporating all the latest features in comfortable seating, efficient heating and diffused lighting. Most of these bodies were built at the Hendon works of the Duple Bodies & Motors Ltd., and one of 'Thackray's Way' first batch of coaches featured in Duple publicity of the period. Most of the coaches were fitted with a roof-mounted luggage pen, reached by a vertical ladder fixed to the rear of the body.

Although the Duple bodies were largely identical, UW 2615/6 had slightly lower set windscreens, and drivers recall they were a bit uncomfortable for taller men to drive as a result.

The company was also fortunate in later having the opportunity to purchase a batch of forward-control Wycombe-bodied Gilford coaches as the result of another operator's financial failure (as will be detailed in due course).

Apart from the above, it also known that a small number of other Gilfords also passed through the Thackrays hands before sale to other nearby concerns such as 'Newbury & District'. It is not clear if they ever considered operating these coaches or were acting purely as dealers.

To keep these vehicles on the road the Reading maintenance staff, at the opening of the Colonnade Garage, consisted of the following:

Ernest Cory	Depot Manager	Went to Firestone Tyres
Jack Holmes	Night Foreman	Ex-London
Mr. Stillman	Chief Electrician	Ex-London
Albert Rackley	Coachpainter/Signwriter	
Albert Moss	Paintshop Hand	Known as 'Moscow'
Bob Davis	Coach Trimmer	
Ted Franklin	Coachbuilder	Known as 'Taffy'
Charlie Tanton	Fitter (Nights)	Former coach operator
George Bridges	Fitter	Ex-Spencers Wood
Jim Boswell	Fitter	Ex-'Thames Valley'
Harold Drinkwater	Fitter	Ex-Spencers Wood
Jack Lovegrove	Fitter	Ex-Milkman
Harry Pullen	Fitter	Ex-Straker Squire
Bertie Wilcox	Fitter	
Jack Davey	Engine/Gearbox Chargehand	
George Hamblin	Engine Fitter/Borer	Ex-Spencers Wood
Tom Lake	Apprentice Fitter	Ex-Spencers Wood
'Nobby' Earley	Apprentice Fitter	Ex-Spencers Wood
Bob Cue	Cleaner	

Amongst the traffic staff at Reading at that time were:

Frank Doddington	Traffic Superintendent	Ex-Spencers Wood
Paddy Cain	Driver	
Trevor Farrant	Driver	
Bill James	Driver	
'Darkie' Naish	Driver	
Herb Nash	Driver	Ex-Spencers Wood
Mr. Ritchie	Driver	Ex-Spencers Wood
Ted Baylis	Driver	Ex-Spencers Wood
Fred Tigwell	Driver	Ex-Spencers Wood
Bill Bishop	Driver	Ex-Jarvis, Reading
Bert Bishop	Driver	Ex-Smith, Reading
Guy Worstiff	Driver	

Although a number of the drivers had previous coach experience, others were recruited from the growing number of men seeking a steady job in those uncertain times. One such recruit was Tom Reader from Winnersh, who joined after trying his hand at chicken farming.

 One of the former Unic taxis became a pick-up truck at the Colonnade, but that was later replaced by a light van based on the Morris 'Cowley' chassis. The garage staff also looked after the regular servicing of Bob Thackray's own car, initially a YO-registered Buick but later a Vauxhall. His son Fred had an Essex, which is recalled as having a horse-shoe with the inscription 'Fobra' adorning its radiator.

Posing with one of the UW-registered Gilfords at The Wharf in Newbury is boy conductor Meredith, together with former Jarvis driver Bill Bishop.

Coach operations at the London premises centred on overnight stabling of vehicles that were exchanged at Reading on a daily basis. When any running repairs were necessary the fitters from the taxi garage could do deal with most tasks. Those traffic staff who were based there are recalled as:

H. J. Buchan	Chief Inspector	Returned to Thackray's
Mr. Pennington	Traffic Superintendent	

Lionel Churchill Driver
Bert Scibbons Driver Known as 'Skimbo'

Mr. Buchan was provided with a secondhand 'TK' registered Morris car as his run-around.

We have already heard how the employees formerly at Spencers Wood came to be working at the Colonnade, and some background is also known on certain others.

Ted Franklin had originated from Stroud in Gloucestershire, although much of his childhood was spent in Swansea, hence his Welsh accent and the nickname 'Taffy'. He had been apprenticed to a carpenter but, due to the depression of the late 1920's, he went to London to seek work. There he got a job with coachbuilders Wilkins, Appsley & Keats in the Latimer Road area. Whilst there he was 'hired out' to the Thackrays at their Ledbury Mews West premises to attend to bodywork on their fleet of about 75 Unic taxis.

Ted found he could earn more working directly for the Thackrays, and with the completion of the Colonnade Garage he was sent down to work on the coaches instead. One job he did, which left its mark on the whole fleet, was making the oval-shaped illuminated 'Thackray' boxes fitted to the front dome of the coaches. He also got the job of oak panelling Bob Thackray's games room at Fords Farm in due course.

After 'Thackray's Way' was sold, he continued working at the Colonnade under 'Thames Valley', but suffered several serious accidents in its employ. During the early days of the war he fell from the ceiling trusses of the Lower Thorn Street garage whist applying black-out material. Then in 1952 he had some two-and-a-half tons of aluminium sheeting topple onto him in the bodyshop at the Colonnade. The latter incident left him partially incapacitated and without adequate compensation.

Charlie Tanton, whose earlier charabanc activities have already been noted, worked on a permanent 5.00pm to 2.00am shift, attending to the coaches routine maintenance and any running repairs to enable use the following day. 'Nobby' Earley or Tom Lake was with him, as they worked various shifts. Charlie was later transferred to Ledbury Mews West to work on the taxis, eventually buying his own cab, thereby going full circle as some taxi work had supplemented his charabanc business in earlier years.

For young 'Nobby' the 8.30pm to 8.30am shifts effectively precluded any social life, but Jack Holmes got him transferred onto a more varied shift pattern once they were settled in at the Colonnade. Shifts varied between 5.00am to 2.00pm, 1.30pm to 10.30pm, 2.00pm to 11.00pm or 5.00pm to 2.00am.

When on days he worked as an assistant fitter, with some spells manning the petrol pumps – the latter duty entailing the logging of any coaches using the facilities for invoicing to its owners. Evening and night duties tended to consist of checking oil and water and fuelling coaches for service the following day. All the Gilford coaches could be put away in the garage at night, being reversed in by the garage staff.

THE LEDBURY TRANSPORT Co., Ltd.,
CROWN COLONNADE,
LONDON ROAD, READING.

THACKRAY'S COACHING STATION

REGULAR DAILY SERVICES

NEWBURY — READING — MAIDENHEAD — SLOUGH — LONDON
MAIDENHEAD — HURLEY — HENLEY.

KNOWN AS

THACKRAY'S WAY

The main part of the Ledbury Transport Company letterhead of 1930.

As if one nickname was not enough, young Maurice Earley was also called 'Curly' by Bob Thackray! But he enjoyed working for the Thackrays, and was well thought of. Indeed, in January 1933, he was transferred to the London premises to work on the taxi fleet, where he was once again reunited with Charlie Tanton. There he had responsibility for ten cabs and, as he had recently obtained a PSV Driver's License, he would also act as spare driver for the coaches.

In London he lodged with driver Lionel Churchill, before obtaining his own lodgings in Shepherds Bush. Later he moved out to Hayes and then Southall, finally returning to Reading in 1938.

Shortly after he arrived in London the process of replacing the Unic taxis with new blue and black liveried Austins had begun, at the rate of some 10-20 per year. Sometimes when 'Nobby' came home to Spencers Wood for the weekend he would deposit one of the old taxis at Fords Farm – where, it seems, they were largely left to rot away. He also did some breakdown recovery work at the London end.

His coach driving duties soon settled down to about three trips per week, which was useful overtime, whilst in the summer months he would drive a relief coach as far as Maidenhead when loadings were heavy. Whilst returning from weekends visiting Spencers Wood on the 11.00pm coach, he would take over from the regular driver at Kensington High Street if they needed to get home before transport finished.

About 1936 'Nobby' left 'Thackray's' to work as a fitter with the London Cab Company at Shepherds Bush, where he was again on the 5.00pm to 2.00 am shift. At weekends he continued to do some coach driving for 'Garner's Coaches' of Ealing, 'Valiant Direct' of Ealing or 'Silver Grey' of Reading (where he had family connections by then). With the storm clouds of war gathering, he decided he would rather be in Reading, taking up employment with 'Silver Grey'. That operator was taken over 'Smith's Coaches' of Reading in February 1939, and he passed to them as well. He was to spend 45 years with that operator, most of them as Chief Engineer, but that's another story!

A number of members of the Thackray family also held positions at various times, and they undeniably contributed to the success of the business.

Ben Thackray's son George undertook an engineering apprenticeship at Rolls Royce. He duly joined the London end of the family business, including a spell driving the pirate buses. Later he served as a 'jumping' Inspector on the coaches, in an attempt to stamp out the widespread fiddling by conductors, and in connection with this he was nicknamed 'The Black Prince'. He became the manager of the London taxis in the mid '30's.

Bob's daughter Vera went into the Colonnade offices on leaving school, but (in her own words) was 'hopeless' at such work. After a while she left to concentrate on her love of horses by starting a riding school for children at Fords Farm. Indeed, she became quite famous in riding circles, gaining fourth place in the World Open Championship held at Olympia in June 1931 on her favourite horse 'Don'.

Vera did, however, later have some more involvement in the business, when she later purchased some cabs on an investment basis.

Bob's sister Lizzie, by then known as Elizabeth Deighton, also worked in the Registered Office for a time during the '30's.

Adverse operating conditions, such as this flood at Christchurch Green in Reading, were a frequent hazard in the area traversed by the services.

 Chapter Ten The Pack Re-shuffled

Chapter Ten The Pack Re-shuffled

In the meantime the Thackrays had been considering further expansion, as well as the viability of their existing operations.

It should also be appreciated that legislation then proceeding through Parliament would bring about many changes relating to the licensing of both services and vehicles. It was also widely considered that existing operators would, in general, be allowed to keep services already started – so the race was on to set up new routes before the Road Traffic Act 1930 came into force!

At the Reading Borough Council Hackney Carriage Sub-committee meeting of 17th June 1930 consideration was given to 'Thackray's' application for six more licenses each for the Reading–Newbury and Reading–London routes, together with six each for proposed routes Reading–Camberley and Reading–Bucklebury Common. The latter route could be seen as yet another feeder for the London express, perhaps at the suggestion of driver Trevor Farrant (who hailed from that village)? However, the Camberley route was quite a different matter.

'Thames Valley' served both Bucklebury Common (where it had a dormy shed and a bus was kept overnight) and Camberley, the latter by two different routes, so it is perhaps not surprising that those applications were turned down. It is also interesting to note that the Thackrays did not have enough vehicles to cover those routes anyway!

However, it seems likely that Bob Thackray had expected the other licenses to go through, in view of the opening of the coaching station, He therefore sought another meeting with the Sub-committee, bringing with him further proposals.

At a meeting held on 22nd July 1930 he offered to withdraw all his buses from the Reading–Odiham road on condition that the licences could be transferred onto vehicles to be used on a new Reading–London service to be routed via Wokingham, Bracknell, Ascot and Staines. He also stated that a further six licenses would be required in order to cover the proposed headway, adding that the service would terminate at the coach station rather than entering the town centre. As it was the site was well served by the corporation trams and various bus services.

The Council agreed to these proposals, though they would not be moved by his appeals in respect of the Camberley or Bucklebury Common services. Eleven licenses were granted in respect of the new London service, and once that was concluded the company placed the following two announcements in the 'Reading Standard' edition of 26th July 1930:

'The Ledbury Transport Co. Ltd., 5/6 Crown Colonnade, Reading, known as Thackray's Way, wish to inform the public that their coaches in service on the following routes – Reading, Spencers Wood, Swallowfield, Riseley, Heckfield, Hook, Odiham and Farley Hill will cease to operate after Wednesday 30th July 1930'

'The Ledbury Transport Co. Ltd., 5/6 Crown Colonnade, Reading, known as Thackray's Way, beg to inform the public that, on and after Thursday 31st July 1930, a service of Cream and Red Saloon Coaches will operate between Reading and London with an hourly service via Winnersh, Wokingham, Binfield, Bracknell, Ascot. Sunningdale, Virginia Water, Egham and Staines at the following times:
Weekdays and Sundays these coaches will leave Thackray's Coach Station, Crown Colonnade, London Road, Reading – first coach leaves Reading 7.20am, last coach leaves Reading 8.20pm. First coach leaves London (Oxford Circus) 9.45am, last coach leaves London 10.45pm.'

It would have been interesting to be a fly on the wall in the 'Thames Valley' offices that day! For whatever TV's directors had thought of events on the Bath Road, there is no doubt that the company was completely taken by surprise by this latest move by the Thackrays.

Not that TV did anything immediately, but for 'Safeway' it spelt the end, with its service ceasing on 26th August 1930.

Additional support was, however, forthcoming for the new service from Wokingham Borough Council. For some time there had been calls for the 'Southern Railway' to improve its rather slow and poorly-stocked service to Waterloo, but the railway effectively never did anything until the line was electrified in 1938! The Council therefore welcomed 'Thackray's Way' with open arms, and in future times it was to prove to be a useful ally.

The journey time for the service through Ascot was the same 2 hours and 12 minutes as scheduled for the route along the Bath Road.

The first timetable for the new service through Ascot, showing fares tables.

SPECIAL NOTICE

On and After
JULY 31st, 1930

An Hourly Service of our Cream and Red Super Saloon Coaches will be in operation between

Reading and London

starting from our Coach Station, London Road, Reading,

Via WINNERSH, WOKINGHAM, BINFIELD, BRACKNELL, ASCOT, SUNNINGHILL, SUNNINGDALE, EGHAM, STAINES, LONDON (Oxford Circus)

Reading First Coach 7.20 a.m. Reading Last Coach 8.20 p.m.
London First Coach 9.45 a.m. London Last Coach 10.45 p.m.

FARES. Single Tickets Only.

London to	Fare	Reading to	Fare
Staines	1/6	Winnersh	6d.
Egham	1/6	Embrook	6d.
Sunninghill	1/9	Wokingham	6d.
Sunningdale	1/9	Binfield	1/-
Ascot	1/9	Bracknell	1/-
Bracknell	1/9	Ascot	1/6
Binfield	1/9	Sunninghill	1/6
Wokingham	2/-	Sunningdale	1/6
Embrook	2/-	Egham	1/9
Winnersh	2/-	Staines	1/9
Reading	2/-	London	2/-

 In order to cover the service via Ascot all the Gilford coaches on the Reading–Newbury route were transferred onto the service, together with other new Gilfords that had been temporarily employed on Sunday excursions to Southsea. Roof-mounted side route-boards were introduced, some having a large 'ASCOT' painted in the centre, presumably to avoid confusion with the service via the Bath Road, whilst small boards indicating the same were carried above the front windscreen. Prior to that the coaches had carried the main place-names of the Reading-Maidenhead-London route painted on the glass rain-shields above the side windows.

The route via Maidenhead was shown in timetables as 'Route 1' and that via Ascot as 'Route 2', though no route numbers were carried on the coaches. Unusually, however, the coaches did carry commercial adverts on the rear panels.

To take their place buses previously employed on the Reading–Odiham route, together with the ex-Hope and Tanton coaches were placed on the Newbury service.

The Newbury route called for six vehicles and was covered by ex-'Pride of the Valley' Thornycrofts OT 1339 and HO 6335 and Chevrolets RX 1456 and RX 1590, together with others selected from the ex-Hope Lancia DP 3???, Dennis DP 3590, Delahaye DP 7669 and ex-Tanton Gilfords RD 1886 and VM 8638. Whilst it may be purely speculative to imply that all saw service, it is interesting to note the following item that appeared as a result of an early 'Omnibus Society' tour which visited the area at the time:

'Despite the impression in London that all 'Thackray's' coaches are splendid normal-control Gilfords, he has many strange but well kept vehicles on the Reading-Newbury service. Among the less expected cars were a Chevrolet 4-wheeler, ditto 6-wheeler, a Thornycroft bus of about 1925, and a very old Dennis chara. Thackray has a fine garage in Reading at which overhauls are performed. A Gilford coach, minus engine, was seen within, and a 'Morning Star' coach was parked there – presumably a 'spare' on the London–Bristol run.'

Again though others were drawn to the fray, with the 'London General' registering a subsidary 'Green Line Coaches' on 9th July 1930, with the express intent of starting or competing over routes into the metropolis from the surrounding countryside. The established Windsor–London route passed to the new company, whilst 1930 saw a number of routes commencing or licensing applications lodged with Local Authorities. Those of relevance to this story involved the commencement of a Charing Cross–Sunningdale route (hourly, but soon increased to half-hourly) from 23rd July 1930 and a Charing Cross–Maidenhead service from 2nd August 1930. The Windsor service had the effect of ousting initially 'Highways' from July 1930, though they returned in November of that year.

'Green Line' also lodged applications with Reading and Wokingham Borough Councils, the former for a route via the Bath Road and the latter by way of Ascot and the established Sunningdale service. Reading refused outright, whereas the Council at Wokingham deferred the matter pending enactment of the 1930 Road Traffic Act. That action undoubtably included a measure of goodwill in favour of the Thackrays.

There is also little doubt that 'London General' had targeted the Thackray operation as one it would like to defeat, and one wonders if someone there remembered that they had earlier run pirate buses against them?

Whereas both the Reading–Newbury and Reading–Maidenhead–London services carried conductors, the new service via Ascot was operated as a pre-booked seat service from the outset.

One effect of the additional service was the slight reduction on the route via Maidenhead, which was reduced from thirty three to twenty nine trips daily, but that was done by removing some poorly-patronised timings.

The Newbury service was also slightly rearranged, and for the first time a vehicle was out-stationed in the town to allow some earlier short-workings between Newbury and Thatcham to provide transport to the Colthrop Board Mills, prior to taking up duties on the full route. Quite where the vehicle was kept has not been established, but in view of certain forthcoming events it is likely that it was kept at the premises of Andrews & Son in Northcroft Lane. Several of the drivers already lived at Thatcham, so it seems likely that they covered the duty.

The revised Newbury service required only three vehicles to cover the schedules, and the other two were temporarily kept at the Castle Street premises, an arrangement that continued until the end of that Summer. By then it was no longer necessary to park vehicles at Vincent's Station Hill yard.

At that time the Reading town centre terminus of the Reading–Maidenhead–London was moved from St.Mary's Butts to the Palace Theatre parking ground. This is understood to be part of Bob Thackray's offer to appease the Council, which was at that time squeezing operators out of that location. It was also about this time that the Newbury terminus was relocated at The Wharf, and this came about through a similar desire by the Council in that town to keep the streets clear of parked buses and the numerous carrier's vans.

At this point in time the Company employed 29 drivers, all of which were licensed with the various local authorities to drive on all services.

During early Autumn 1930 it became possible to consider the fate of the remaining buses and coaches inherited from absorbed operators. As it was, since the departure from the Castle Street premises, such motley vehicles had been kept at the Colonnade and were therefore in the gaze of the travelling public. That Bob Thackray felt concerned about this matter is evidenced by the fact that he actually responded to the Omnibus Society regarding its earlier report:

'Thackray's Way', which is operated by the Ledbury Transport Co. Ltd., of Crown Colonnade, Reading, point out that the non-standard vehicles of which we referred to earlier, have been withdrawn from all services and disposed of. Gilford 26-seat saloons are now standard. The Reading premises include Booking Office, Waiting Room, Restaurant for 200, Cloak Rooms and Parking for 100 coaches. As the Bath, Oxford and two roads to London join here and all coaches passing through Reading pass the point, one can see a very busy future for it. Practically all day, buses run via Maidenhead every 30 minutes and via Ascot hourly from London to Reading, while 'Thackray's' also work a 30-minute service to Newbury. Some time ago, the Reading–Riseley service of Mr. Cordery was purchased, and that was the source of the mixed fleet referred to.'

A variety of fates awaited the withdrawn stock. The former Hope Lancia, together with ex- Tanton Gilfords RD 1886 and VM 8638 were all sold to

 Andrews of Newbury, who traded under the name of 'Favourite Coaches'. The ex-Hope Dennis DP 3590 was disposed of by December 1930, but its fate is not known, whilst the Delahaye replaced the former Ireland GMC as the breakdown wagon from early 1931.

Thornycroft OT 1339 was also disposed of to an unknown location, whereas Thornycroft HO 6335 lingered on in the yard at the Colonnade, had its seats removed and became a painter's store until finally disposed of in May 1933. The 4-wheel Chevrolet (RX 1590) became a goods vehicle with Ben Smith of Wantage, but the 6-wheeler was to see further service with Thackrays before final sale. Initially it was taken to Fords Farm at Calcot, where the body was de-mounted nearby the Calcot mill pool, becoming a convenient changing-room for Bob's children who liked to swim there! This was later replaced by purpose-built changing rooms.

Former Cordery Thornycroft HO 6335 and former Hope Delahaye chara DP 7669 await their fates at the side of the Colonnade yard in late 1930.

The chassis of RX 1456 then received a platform body, in order to tulfil its new role as a petrol bowser. It had been found that the Gilfords could not do a full day on the London run on one tank of petrol, and with the loss of the Castle Street facility, it became necessary to have a supply available at the Palace Theatre parking ground. This was arranged by filling 5-gallon cans at the Colonnade, then loaded onto the Chevrolet and driven into Reading for topping up coaches each afternoon. This practice was used for a year or so, after which the Chevrolet became a lorry with W. G. Cook of Theale and coaches were changed off instead.

'Premier' once again posed a threat, when they attempted to gain 11 licenses from both Reading and Wokingham Borough Councils during September 1930. Wokingham refused to deal with the matter pending the commencement of the Road Traffic Act, whilst Reading did not approve the licenses.

Another threat came from an altogether different source in September, when Reading Borough Council found itself in receipt of a petition complaining of night-time disturbance caused by maintenance work at the Colonnade garage. Thirty five residents from Granby Gardens, London Road, De Beauvoir Road, Wokingham Road and Carnarvon Road had signed the petition asking the Council to act. However, it had no powers to do so, and nothing further is heard of the matter.

As the services were still developing to cater for the needs of the travelling public, some further detailed changes took place from October 1930 on the Reading-Maidenhead-London service. The first journey of the day from Reading at 6.00am, and that from London at 7.30am, were discontinued due to lack of custom. This, and some minor amendments elsewhere, allowed the vehicle commitment to be reduced from ten to nine coaches, three of which continued to be kept at Ledbury Mews West and were exchanged on a daily basis. One spare coach was also kept at the London end, to cover vehicle failure or for relief work if required.

Indeed, the coaches were kept busy, with only seven of the twenty four not required to cover the schedules. Four covered the Reading-Ascot-London route, all of which were based at Reading, nine were on the Reading-Maidenhead-London route (with four kept in London), whilst four were based in Reading for the service to Newbury.

Further competition appeared on the Slough–London section from Monday 1st October 1930, when 'Premier' introduced a London (The Aldwych)–

THACKRAY'S WAY

READING (Butts) **AND LONDON via Maidenhead.**

Weekdays and Sundays.

London to Reading.

London	Coln-brook	Slough 56 High St	Maiden-head	Reading
A.M.	A.M.	A.M.	A.M.	A.M.
8.0	9.6	9.18	9.36	10.12
9.0	10.6	10.18	10.36	11.12
9.30	10.36	10.48	11.6	11.42
10.0	11.6	11.18	11.36	12.12
10.30	11.36	11.48	12.6	12.42
11.0	12.6	12.18	12.36	1.12
11.30	12.36	12.48	1.6	1.42
12.0	1.6	1.18	1.36	2.12
12.30	1.36	1.48	2.6	2.42
1.0	2.6	2.18	2.36	3.12
1.30	2.36	2.48	3.6	3.42
2.0	3.6	3.18	3.36	4.12
2.30	3.36	3.48	4.6	4.42
3.0	4.6	4.18	4.36	5.12
3.30	4.36	4.48	5.6	5.42
4.0	5.6	5.18	5.36	6.12
4.30	5.36	5.48	6.6	6.42
5.0	6.6	6.18	6.36	7.12
5.30	6.36	6.48	7.6	7.42
6.0	7.6	7.18	7.36	8.12
6.30	7.36	7.48	8.6	8.42
7.0	8.6	8.18	8.36	9.12
7.30	8.36	8.48	9.6	9.42
8.0	9.6	9.18	9.36	10.12
8.30	9.36	9.48	10.6	10.42
9.0	10.6	10.18	10.36	11.12
9.30	10.36	10.48	11.6	11.42
10.30	11.36	11.48	12.6	12.42
11.30	12.36	12.48	1.6	1.42

Reading to London.

Reading	Maiden-head	Slough Town Hall	Coln-brook	London
A.M.	A.M.	A.M.	A.M.	A.M.
7.15	7.51	8.9	8.21	9.27
8.0	8.36	8.54	9.6	10.12
8.30	9.6	9.24	9.36	10.42
9.0	9.36	9.54	10.6	11.12
9.30	10.6	10.24	10.36	11.42
10.0	10.36	10.54	11.6	12.12
10.30	11.6	11.24	11.36	12.42
11.0	11.36	11.54	12.6	1.12
11.30	12.6	12.24	12.36	1.42
12.0	12.36	12.54	1.6	2.12
12.30	1.6	1.24	1.36	2.42
1.0	1.36	1.54	2.6	3.12
1.30	2.6	2.24	2.36	3.42
2.0	2.36	2.54	3.6	4.12
2.30	3.6	3.24	3.36	4.42
3.0	3.36	3.54	4.6	5.12
3.30	4.6	4.24	4.36	5.42
4.0	4.36	4.54	5.6	6.12
4.30	5.6	5.24	5.36	6.42
5.0	5.36	5.54	6.6	7.12
5.30	6.6	6.24	6.36	7.42
6.0	6.36	6.54	7.6	8.12
6.30	7.6	7.24	7.36	8.42
7.0	7.36	7.54	8.6	9.12
7.30	8.6	8.24	8.36	9.42
8.0	8.36	8.54	9.6	10.12
9.0	9.36	9.54	10.6	11.12
10.0	10.36	10.54	11.6	12.12
11.0	11.36	11.54	12.6	1.12

PRIVATE HIRE A SPECIALITY.

THACKRAY'S WAY

LONDON TO READING (Colonnade) **via Ascot.**

Weekdays and Sundays.

London	H'smith	Staines	Egham	Sun'hill	Ascot	Bra'knel	Binfield	Wok'ham	Embrook	Winnersh	Reading
A. M.	A. M.	A. M.	A. M.	A. M.	A. M.	A. M.	A. M.	A. M.	A. M.	A. M.	A. M.
9 45	1010	1051	1057	1111	1116	1125	1131	1141	1146	1151	1157
1045	1110	1151	1157	1211	1216	1225	1231	1241	1246	1251	1257
1145	1210	1251	1257	1 11	1 16	1 25	1 31	1 41	1 46	1 51	1 57
1245	1 10	1 51	1 57	2 11	2 16	2 25	2 31	2 41	2 46	2 51	2 57
2 45	3 10	3 51	3 57	4 11	4 16	4 25	4 31	4 41	4 46	4 51	4 57
3 45	4 10	4 51	4 57	5 11	5 16	5 25	5 31	5 41	5 46	5 51	5 57
4 45	5 10	5 51	5 57	6 11	6 16	6 25	6 31	6 41	6 46	6 51	6 57
5 45	6 10	6 51	6 57	7 11	7 16	7 25	7 31	7 41	7 46	7 51	7 57
7 45	8 10	8 51	8 57	9 11	9 16	9 25	9 31	9 41	9 46	9 51	9 57
*8 45	9 10	9 51	9 57	1011	1016	1025	1031	1041	1046	1051	1057
9 45	1010	1051	1057	1111	1116	1125	1131	1141	1146	1151	1157
*1045	1110	1151	1157	1211	1216	1225	1231	1241	1246	1251	1257

* Sundays only.

READING (Colonnade) **TO LONDON via Ascot.**

Reading	Winnersh	Embrook	Wok'ham	Binfield	Bra'knel	Ascot	Sun'hill	Egham	Staines	H'smith	London
A. M.	A. M.	A. M.	A. M.	A. M.	A. M.	A. M.	A. M.	A. M.	A. M.	A. M.	A. M.
7 20	7 26	7 31	7 36	7 46	7 52	8 1	8 6	8 20	8 26	9 7	9 32
8 20	8 26	8 31	8 36	8 46	8 52	9 1	9 6	9 20	9 26	10 7	1032
9 20	9 26	9 31	9 36	9 46	9 52	10 1	10 6	1020	1026	11 7	1132
1020	1026	1031	1036	1046	1052	11 1	11 6	1120	1126	12 7	1232
1220	1226	1231	1236	1246	1252	1 1	1 6	1 20	1 26	2 7	2 32
1 20	1 26	1 31	1 36	1 46	1 52	2 1	2 6	2 20	2 26	3 7	3 32
2 20	2 26	2 31	2 36	2 46	2 52	3 1	3 6	3 20	3 26	4 7	4 32
3 20	3 26	3 31	3 36	3 46	3 52	4 1	4 6	4 20	4 26	5 7	5 32
5 20	5 26	5 31	5 36	5 46	5 52	6 1	6 6	6 20	6 26	7 7	7 32
*6 20	6 26	6 31	6 36	6 46	6 52	7 1	7 6	7 20	7 26	8 7	8 32
7 20	7 26	7 31	7 36	7 46	7 52	8 1	8 6	8 20	8 26	9 7	9 32
*8 20	8 26	8 31	8 36	8 46	8 52	9 1	9 6	9 20	9 26	10 7	1032

* Sundays only.

81 *Timetables for both London services from the November 1930 edition are shown at 90% of original size. The fare table from the same time will be found elsewhere in this chapter.*

 Farnham Common service. That service fared so well that it was increased in frequency to 15 minutes from 5th February 1931. By that date the Slough-London section was being covered by no fewer than 17 coaches per hour in the ownership of four operators, perhaps one of the most intensively served coach routes of that time.

Also from 1st October 1930 'Thames Valley' added a fifth vehicle to the Reading-Ascot-London route, providing an hourly headway from 7.30am to 8.30pm from Reading, with returning journeys from 10.00am to 11.00pm.

The Reading-based employees had the benefit of a thriving Social Club, the secretary being Maurice Wigley. During November 1930 he booked the Large Town Hall for a dance to be held in January 1931 in aid of the Queen Victoria Nursing Institute.

A further revised timetable came into operation from November 1930. No changes were made to the London service via Maidenhead, though the route via Ascot had perhaps not lived up to expectations. The weekday departures from Reading at 6.20pm and 9.20pm, together with the return journeys from London at 8.45pm and 11.45pm were withdrawn, although the 6.20pm departure was retained for Sundays only.

Out-stationing at Newbury also ceased, and the first coach left Reading at 6.45am, with an hourly service until 12.45pm, followed by a 30-minute headway throughout the rest of the day until the last departure from Newbury at 11.45pm. On Saturdays and Sundays some extra journeys were added, though Sunday operations started a little later in the morning.

One result of the revised arrangements of the Newbury service was the discontinuation of the short-workings between Newbury and the Colthrop Board Mills near Thatcham. Andrews of Newbury evidently took over that role, though it is not known if there had been any dialogue with the Thackrays over the matter. 'Thames Valley' also provided similar short-workings on its Route 10 (Reading-Newbury) using two double-deckers based at its large shed in Mill Lane, Newbury.

However, the era of unbridled competition, which itself had been made even more unpredictable by local variations in hackney carriage licensing was about to be brought to a sudden end. The Road Traffic Act, 1930 was to take effect from 1st January 1931, and with it came a new licensing system controlled by Regional Traffic Commissioners through a system of formal applications, which were heard against other operator's objections, and the ability to remove licenses where conditions were not met. The construction and fitness for service of public service vehicles would also be controlled, with regular inspections taking place, and powers to take vehicles off the road. Taxicabs and hire-cars were, however, omitted and remained subject to the old hackney carriage regulations.

This close-up view of Gilford no.2 (GP 5139) shows that the fleet was maintained to a high standard.

In reality, the conscientious operator, with a well-maintained fleet, had little to fear from the new legislation. However, many were doubtless daunted by the additional paperwork generated by the new system and the requirement to attend the Traffic Commissioner's Hearings, which could be held at some distance from the operator's base.

THACKRAY'S WAY

FARES.

LONDON (Oxford C.) to	Single.	Ret.
Colnbrook	1/3	2/6
Slough 56 High St	1/6	3/-
Maidenhead (High Street)	1/9	3/6
Twyford	2/-	4/-
Reading (Butts)	2/-	4/-
Newbury	3/-	6/-
READING (Butts) to		
Twyford	10d	1/8
Maidenhead (High Street)	10d	1/8
Slough Town Hall	1/3	2/6
Colnbrook	1/6	3/-
London (Ox. Cir.)	2/-	4/-
Newbury	1/8	2/-
NEWBURY to		
Reading (Butts)	1/8	2/.
Maidenhead (High Street)	1/9	3/6
Slough Town Hall	2/-	4/-
London (Ox. Cir.)	3/-	6/-

READING (Colonnade) to	Single.	Ret.
Winnersh	9d	1/-
Wokingham	9d	1/-
Binfield	11d	1/6
Bracknell	1/1	1/8
Ascot	1/5	2/-
Blacknest	1/6	-
Sunninghill	1/6	-
Virginia Water	1/9	2/6
Egham	1/9	3/6
Staines	1/9	3/6
London (Ox. Cir.)	2/-	4/-
LONDON to		
Staines	1/9	2/6
Egham	2/-	3/-
Viginia Water	2/-	3/6
Blacknest	2/-	3/6
Sunninghill	2/-	3/6
Ascot	2/-	3/6
Bracknell	2/-	3/6
Binfield	2/-	3/6
Wokingham	2/-	4/-
Winnersh	2/-	4/-
Reading (Col'ade)	2/-	4/-

PALACE THEATRE

Telephone **READING** **920**

Two Performances Nightly

6.45 and 8.50

No Telephone Bookings for Saturdays or Bank Holidays

THACKRAY'S COACHES Park on the Palace Ground.

Fares tables in operation at November 1930.

Chapter Eleven The Act Takes Effect

As it would not be practical for the Traffic Commissioners to review all licence applications immediately, existing operators were permitted to continue running over the roads they served until the relevant hearing took place. Also, any services introduced between 1st January and 8th February 1931 would also be permitted until applications could be dealt with.

However, there was no rush by 'Thackray's Way' to stake any further claims before the deadline, though it did seek a route diversion from Wokingham Borough Council in December 1930. The intention was to run the Reading-London service via Oxford Road and Station Road, before rejoining the Reading Road at Shute End. This was presumably in order to pass by the railway station, as the Oxford Road had recently become a through road. In the event, the Council refused the diversion.

Also rather surprisingly, in view of the impending effects of The Act, 'Thames Valley' actually reduced its workings on the Reading-Ascot-London service, with a varied number of journeys on different days from 1st January 1931. This schedule only required three or four cars to cover, but should perhaps be considered as only a seasonal adjustment.

Indeed, TV returned to a full hourly service from 1st July 1931, on a schedule worked by five Reading-based cars.

As part of the run up to the Traffic Commissioner's Hearings for the area the Local Authorities were given an opportunity to make recommendations for the continuation (or otherwise) of services formerly within thier juristriction.

Reading Borough Council wrote on 24th March 1931 in support of the applications for 'Thackray's' services on Reading-Maidenhead-London, Reading-Ascot-London and Reading-Newbury. Wokingham Borough also made its feelings known, supporting the 'Thackray's' service through that town, but asking the Traffic Commissioner to refuse the 'Premier' application. The latter operator was becoming embroiled in financial difficulties, which would inevitable lead to a deterioration in the standard of care for its coaches.

 As it was, ‘Premier’ effectively sealed its own fate, when it continued operating other services illegally whilst it lodged appeals. Many of the Commissioners came from military backgrounds, and such impudence was not to be tolerated!

The Traffic Commissioner held the hearings in respect of those services at Reading on 27th April 1931, with the results being published in ‘Notices & Proceedings’ on 15th May. The Reading-Newbury and Reading-Maidenhead-London licenses were granted, subject to certain conditions. The application had sought to make St. Mary’s Butts the terminal point for the service from Newbury, but the Commissioner insisted on continuation of the use of the Palace Theatre Parking Ground. However, the application for the Reading-Ascot-London license was refused!

Gilford GC 1867 enters the Colonnade Coaching Station from the service via Ascot in late 1930. The loss of this route was an unexpected blow.

Looking at it objectively, it is evident that the Commissioner found in favour of ‘Thames Valley’ as being the originator of that route. However, the Thackray’s were not happy with this decision and an appeal was lodged. At its meeting of 4th June Wokingham Borough Council agreed to write to the Commissioner in support of the service.

87 One of the coaches was assigned a special role on 20th April 1931, when it served as the wedding transport for George Thackray and his bride Alice Timberlake who married in West London. Inspector Edwardes was on hand to ensure all went smoothly, and he issued the newlywed Alice with a ticket endorsed 'Mrs. George Thackray First Ride'. The ticket duly survived forgotten in an old handbag until rediscovered by daughter Lily many years later!

The other objectors to the recent applications were Reading Borough Council, in respect of the use of St. Mary's Butts as a terminus for the Newbury route, and both the 'Southern' and 'Great Western' railways against all the services other those of the associated 'Thames Valley'!

The loss of the route via Ascot was indeed a blow to 'Thackray's Way', so it must have been a bitter disappointment when the appeal failed n 28th August 1931. The matter was reported to Wokingham BC on 3rd September 1931, with the result that the Town Clerk was instructed to write to the Minister of Transport and the local MP General Clifton-Brown. Despite the above, including questions asked in the House of Commons, no overturning of the decision took place. However, the Thackray's did not let the matter rest, and they submitted a fresh application for consideration by the Traffic Commissioner on 4th December 1931. Again WBC showed its support by sending a deputation to talk to the Chairman of the Traffic Commissioners prior to the meeting.

It should also be noted that an unsuccessful appellant would incur the costs of the hearing, whilst any objectors would face no such risk.

Later in December WBC received another letter informing them that the new application had also been refused, and thanking the councillors for the support shown. And, so Wokingham saw the last of its direct link by the coaches of 'Thackray's Way' with London.

Apart from the decision to license individual operators on particular routes, the Commissioners also had the power to enforce co-operation between operators sharing the same route. These powers were invoked in respect of the Reading-Newbury road, previously worked by the services of both 'Thames Valley' and 'Thackray's Way', as the route had been deemed to be a Stage Carriage Service.

88 *Expansion took place at Ledbury Mews West in 1932, when further mews cottages and stables to the left of this photo were acquired. This view was taken through the archway entrance from Ledbury Road, with the taxi garage building to the right.*

The Commissioners imposed a joint timetable and common fares on the route from 30th June 1931. The operational basis was split at one-third to 'Thackray's' and two-thirds to TV, so again it would appear that the first established operator was indeed treated more favourably. This resulted in a timetable calling for three TV Leyland 'Titan' TD1 double-deckers and just two 'Thackray's' Gilford coaches, one of the latter only taking up duties at midday. Despite the fares being standardised, there was no inter-availability of tickets between the two companies. Even so, TV actually lodged an unsuccessful appeal, in the hope of regaining sole operation. As it was neither operator included the other's journeys in its timetables for until some years later!

The TV General Manager T. Graham Homer reported at the end of June 1931 that the 'Thackray's' competition was costing it some £16,000 per annum!

Another 'association' with a local motor business came about on Wednesday 2nd September 1931, when Bob's daughter Edna married Wilf Julian. His family had developed a successful garage and car dealership business in Reading.

From September 1931 fares on the Reading-Maidenhead-London route, together with those of competing services sharing common sections from Maidenhead onwards, were also fixed by the Commissioners, bringing to an end the 'fares wars' that had sometimes broken out before in the scramble for passengers. This meant that the adult return fare rose from 4 shillings to 5 shillings. The same fare also applied to the TV service via Ascot.

Almost certainly as a direct result of the Road Traffic Act, with all its attendant dealings with the Traffic Commissioners, it was decided to appoint a General Manager. The post was filled by Andre Louis Guilmant, and it has been suggested that the Thackray's bankers may have had a hand in his appointment. Mr. Guilmant and his wife Kate were living in College Road at the time of his appointment, but moved to Kings Road in 1935. For some reason his office was not located in the Registered Office at 5/6 Crown Colonnade, but consisted of a wooden building erected in the yard. From there he managed to keep the operations on the right side of the law. Like Bob Thackray, Mr. Guilmant was an active Mason.

Probably about the same time Maurice Wigley was appointed as Traffic Supervisor at the London end. Both moves were also intended to ensure that 'Thackray's Way' was protected from falling foul of the Act, which was made even more of a necessity through the actions of other concerns. Both 'Green Line' and 'Thames Valley' issued specific instructions to their Inspectors to look for any contravention of the license conditions by 'Thackray's' in order that they could be reported to the Traffic Commissioners.

Joe Challis, the well-known steam traction enthusiast was a regular passenger at the time, coming home to the Reading area at weekends from his work of steam ploughing the market gardens to the west of London. Joe recalls that the coaches were often very full by the time he boarded on the Great West Road, near the present-day Heathrow Airport. However, the conductors appreciated that he had been working hard away all week, so they would let him stand if necessary. Standing was of course strictly not permitted, so Joe would co-operate by lying on the floor when passing through the towns!

The first year of the Road Traffic Act had certainly left the Thackrays feeling a little bruised and battered by the setbacks it had bestowed on their business. So, yet again, it was time to have a rethink on strategy.

One of the most significant developments for the London cab trade was the arrival of purpose-built Austins such as this example. 'Thackray's' soon set about replacing the outdated Unics at a steady rate in the early 1930's.

THACKRAYS WAY

92 On the cab front, 1931 had seen some improvement for operators in London. The Road Traffic Act had succeeded in reducing the number of coaches entering the capital's streets which, when combined with the appointment of a new Minister of Transport, resulted in some of the earlier restrictions being rescinded.

Further improvements, for both operators and passengers alike, came with the acceptance by the Met Police of new purpose-built Austin chassis. This move changed the dominance of cab makes in London in favour of Austin, and a succession of models from that manufacturer entered the 'Thackray's' fleet throughout the '30's.

Overleaf: *Gilford coach GJ1332 does its bit to clear an enormous queue (only about a quarter of which is reproduced here!) from St. Mary's Butts in Reading on the London service. Inspector Doddington is seen to the right, in what was probably a view taken during an Easter weekend.*

Chapter Twelve Connections To All Parts

Still stinging from the loss of the service via Ascot and the restrictions imposed on the Newbury workings, there is little doubt that serious thought was given over the Winter of 1931/2 about measures to redress the balance.

Obviously, there was no hope of regaining the lost route, so ways had to be found of maximising potential traffic on established services and finding other work for the coaches.

Indeed, the fleet actually grew by a further six in August 1932, with the acquisition of a batch of second-hand Gilford 168OT's with 26-seater front-entrance bodies by the associated Wycombe Motor Bodies. These were registered GP 5139-5145 and had been delivered in July 1931 to 'Main Lines' for use on its London-Plymouth service. That operator had failed financially, so the coaches were apparently quite a bargain. They retained their original destination blinds, which included Reading and London, but also featured other further afield places such as Plymouth and Torquay.

One of the former 'Main Lines' Gilfords no.12 (GP 5144) stands in front of part of White's Tea Rooms on the west side of the Colonnade site.

 The GP’s, as they were generally known, become popular workhorses in the fleet, the drivers liking the separate cab, whilst passengers appreciated the extra leg-room in a body length usually having 32 seats. Gruss air suspension was fitted, as were large roof-mounted luggage racks.

However, the Spring of 1932 was overshadowed by a family tragedy. Bob’s son Fred had risen to become the top amateur National Hunt jockey. He entered the Grand National, for the fourth consecutive year on Friday 18th March on second favourite ‘Gregalach’, a horse that had already won the race in 1929. The 10-year old started out well under Fred and looked set for a good win.

At the 12th fence the rider-less ‘Perilous Jack’ cut across the path of the horses as they jumped, decimating the field as a result. Such was the melee that only 8 out of 32 starters reached the final fence that year.

Fred was piled up against the rail and badly trampled. He received injuries to his head and remained in a coma until 31st March. He was never really well again and was dogged by epilepsy as a result. The incident spelt the end of his career riding over the sticks, though he is reputed to have raced on the flat again.

Fred’s family had maintained a bedside vigil and he was eventually allowed home to Calcot on 24th April, travelling in a hammock strung from the railway carriage ceiling in order to minimise jolting to his injuries.

The one silver lining to come from the terrible accident was the marriage of Fred to Anne Devon in 1935. She had been the nurse who looked after him at the Liverpool nursing home where he had been recuperating. A house was built on part of the Fords Farm land and named Wroxham, with access from Mill Lane, Calcot, where the couple lived and had their children Brian and Jane.

With his riding career behind him, Fred’s father found him a new role as Manager of the London cab business. He was also made a Director of the ‘Ledbury Transport Co. Ltd.’, though it would be fair to say that he had little real interest in either business. Indeed, he spent little time in London, with day-to-day matters remaining in the hands of his cousin George.

 The presence at the Ledbury Mews West site was increased from 1932, with the acquisition of further mews properties. George Thackray duly went to live at No.3, with the coach-painter Johnny Warnes living opposite. As part of the expansion, former tenant W. Darby was evidently relocated to the Scampston Mews premises.

Although some advertised excursions and private hire work had been undertaken throughout the company's existence, it was decided to apply for licenses under the new Act for a programme of excursions and tours. Some were to the coastal resorts of Bognor, Southsea, Bournemouth, Southampton and Brighton, for operation between Easter and September. Others were to specific events, with excursions to Thame Show, horse-racing at Ascot and Epsom, motor-racing at Brooklands, the Hendon Air Show as well as the very popular Aldershot Military Tattoo held in the evenings during June.

The starting place for the excursions was the Palace Theatre Parking Ground, but when the hearing was held in Portsmouth between 5th to 7th July 1932 none of the coastal destinations were granted. Although the other licenses were granted, restrictions were imposed on days of operation and the maximum number of coaches permitted, these measures being a response to the objections voiced on the part of the other established Reading coach operators many of whom regarded 'Thackray's' as intruders.

However, despite the foregoing, a further successful application was made in early August, which allowed the addition of excursions to Hayling Island and Lee-on-Solent. A circular tour from Reading via Aldermaston, Kingsclere, Overton, Whitchurch, Stockbridge, Romsey, Cadnam, Lyndhurst, Lymington, then back through Lyndhurst, Totton, Southampton, Winchester and Basingstoke, was added and made a very pleasant day out.

As regards the London service, it was decided to develop feeder services, the first of which was between Maidenhead and Henley, by way of Maidenhead Thicket, Burchetts Green, Hurley and Remenham Hill. This commenced on Monday 5th September 1932, with eight weekday journeys from Maidenhead (Shoppenhangers Road) at 8.00am, 10.10am, 12.10pm, 2.10pm. 3.50pm, 5.40pm, 7.40pm and 9.10pm. The journey time was 27 minutes, and on Saturdays and Sundays a later coach ran from Maidenhead at 10.40pm one-way only, whilst the Sunday schedule omitted the first return journey.

The timings had been chosen to afford a good connection with the London service at Maidenhead, making it possible to travel from London to Henley in 2 hours and 7 minutes. The side-mounted route boards were amended to display 'Henley' over the centrally positioned 'Maidenhead' in order to highlight the link.

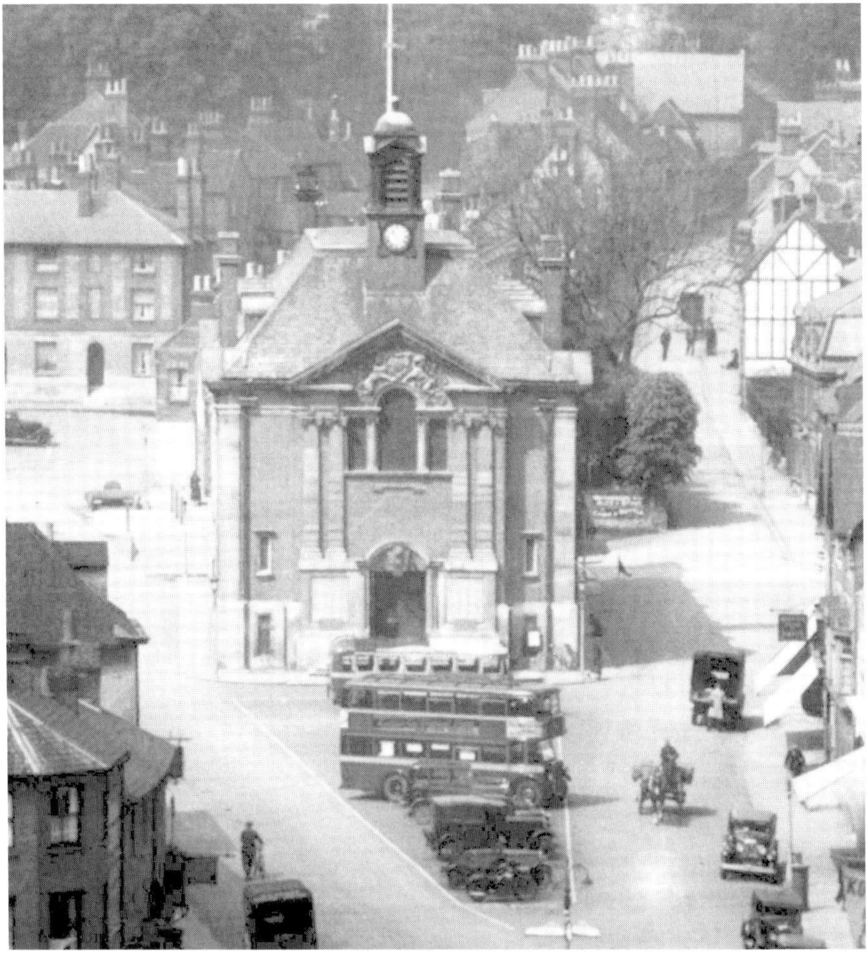

The Henley terminus with a 'Thackray's' Gilford in front of the Town Hall.

TIME TABLES

APRIL 1932

THACKRAY'S WAY

THE LEDBURY TRANSPORT COMPANY, LTD.
5 & 6, Crown Colonnade, Reading. Phone—2673

SUPER SALOON COACHES

Regular Service between

Newbury
Reading
Maidenhead
Slough
Colnbrook
London

All coaches pass the Olympia.

CROWN COLONNADE,
LONDON ROAD, READING.

Garage for 100 Cars.
Repairs and Overhauls.
Day and Night Service.
Lowest Prices.

Front cover of the timetable booklet of April 1932.

97 As the route was also served by Messrs. Fuller & Pomroy's 'Beta Bus Service' between Maidenhead and Hurley, the Traffic Commissioner insisted on co-ordination of fares and timetables. 'Beta' left the route not long after the arrival of 'Thackray's', though it is not clear whether they were bought out or just gave up, as their other bus service (Maidenhead-Binfield) was sold to 'Thames Valley' on 1st April 1933, after which they concentrated on coach work and car hire.

One coach covered the schedule and was out-stationed at Maidenhead. Full details of the arrangements have not come to light, but it is believed that it was kept at the premises of Bob Probets, a long-established coach and taxi (and one time bus) operator in the High Street. Tom Herridge, who it will be recalled was himself a former coach operator before joining 'Thackray's', duly became the regular driver on the duty.

Also on 23rd September 1932 the Traffic Commissioner granted a license for a Wokingham to Wargrave service. This had been partly brought about by continuing dialogue between Bob Thackray and Wokingham Borough Council following the loss of the London service through the town. The service commenced on Saturday 1st October and ran from Wokingham (Station) to Wargrave ('George & Dragon') and was routed via Wokingham (Town Hall), Emmbrook ('Dog & Duck'), Bill Hill Crossroads, Hurst ('The Cricketers') and Twyford (Station).

The service afforded connections with the London service at Twyford, whilst also providing a useful link for villages along the route for journeys to Twyford, Wokingham and points beyond. The route was covered by two coaches based at Reading, one taking up its duties from Twyford at 7.42am, initially with a short-working to Wargrave, before working the through service until it worked from Wargrave to run short to Twyford at 8.12pm. The positioning journey between Reading and Twyford was run 'dead', as was the coach that started its day at Wokingham Station at 7.41am. The latter also finished up at Twyford at 10.17pm before running back to the Colonnade. On Sundays just one coach covered the duty, starting from Wokingham Station at 8.20am and running through until finishing at Twyford at 11.11pm. Les Mullett was a regular driver on the route.

In the meantime 'Thames Valley' had evidently learnt some valuable lessons from the fright that 'Thackray's' had given it on the route via Ascot. Following the trial of Leyland 'Tiger' TS3 car 230, an order was placed for further 'Tigers' for dedicated operation of the Reading-London route. The new TS4 model had superseded the TS3 by then, and TV's car 239 (RX 9307) had the distinction of being the first completed. In fact, it appeared at the November 1931 Commercial Motor Show prior to delivery. It was followed by cars 240/1 (RX 9308/9) in December 1931 and 244 (RX 9541) in February 1932.

The quartet of 'Tigers' were fitted with very well-equipped coach bodies by Brush of Loughborough, and for the first time roof-mounted route boards were used. A distinctive livery of red lower panels, white waistband and black window surrounds and roof was applied, though 244 was finished with red window surrounds and white roof at first. These coaches looked very smart and continued to cover the service until the outbreak of the Second World War. Some of the very similar TS4's from the private hire fleet were also equipped with route board brackets for use on the service if required.

'Thames Valley' car 255 was one of the Tiger TS4's earmarked for use on the Reading-Ascot-London service when required to assist cars 239-41/4. The private hire examples had red roofs, unlike the black used on the four coaches dedicated to the operation.

However, 'Thames Valley' still only ran five return journeys on the weekday schedules, compared with 'Thackray's' twenty six trips. The TV service used Victoria Coach Station, which was more appealing to passengers wishing to book through onto other coach service destinations.

JANUARY 1933

THACKRAY'S WAY

THE LEDBURY TRANSPORT COMPANY, LTD.
5 and 6, Crown Colonnade, Reading. Phone 2673.

WOKINGHAM—WARGRAVE
TIME TABLE

Wokingham Town Hall ..	2 50	4 50	6 50	8 50
Dog & Duck, Embrook ..	2 55	4 55	6 55	8 55
Green Lane Turning ..	2 58	4 58	6 58	8 58
"Castle Inn"	3 2	5 2	7 2	9 2
"Cricketers"	3 5	5 5	7 5	9 5
Twyford Station	3 10	5 10	7 10	9 10
A.A. Box	3 13	5 13	7 13	9 13
Wargrave, George & Dragon	3 17	5 17	7 17	9 17

					s.o.
Wargrave, Grge & Drag.	2 5	4 5	6 5	8 5	10 5
A.A. Box	2 9	4 9	6 9	8 9	10 9
Twyford Station ..	2 12	4 12	6 12	8 12	1012
"Cricketers".. ..	2 17	4 17	6 17	8 17	1017
"Castle Inn" ..	2 20	4 20	6 20	8 20	1020
Green Lane Turning..	2 24	4 24	6 24	8 24	1024
Dog & Duck, Embrook	2 27	4 27	6 27	8 27	1027
Wokingham Town Hall	2 32	4 32	6 32	8 32	1032

s.o.—Sundays only.

FARE CHART

Wargrave, George and Dragon.
Bath Road A.A. Box.

3	3	Twyford.				
4	3	2	Hurst "Cricketers Inn."			
5	4	3	2	Hurst "Castle Inn."		
6	5	4	3	2	Green Lane Turning.	
7	6	5	4	3	2	Embrook, Dog & Duck.
8	7	6	5	4	3	2 Wokingham Town Hall.

Returns:

Wargrave—Wokingham	.. ..	1/3
Hurst	.. ..	8d.
Wokingham—Hurst	.. ..	8d.
Twyford	.. ..	10d.

Children under Fourteen Half Fare.
Season Tickets per Schedule.

The revised routing and timetable for the Wokingham-Wargrave service issued in January 1933.

101 In the light of operational experience, the Wokingham-Wargrave service had its routing amended from 13th January 1933. The coaches thereafter left Wokingham (Town Hall) and proceeded via Matthews Green Road, Toutley Road, Dunt Lane, then through Hurst village by way of Church Lane and School Road.

The revised route certainly took in more of the populated area in and around Hurst, whereas the withdrawal from Wokingham Station may have been forced by the 'Southern Railway' – a company with a financial stake in 'Thames Valley'. Indeed the latter's objections were no doubt influential in the service being reduced to operate in the afternoons and evenings only. So the first departure left Wargrave at 2.05pm and the first return journey from Wokingham was at 2.50pm. Although a two-hour headway was maintained until the 8.50pm departure from the Wokingham end, the viability of the route as a feeder for the London service must surely have been questionable following these revisions. On Sundays the coach actually returned from Wargrave at 10.05pm and ran back to Wokingham, before a 'dead' journey back along the A329 to its garage in Reading.

Other licenses applied for on 13th January were for excursions and tours for the 1933 season. Again, experience had shown that the most popular seaside destinations were already well served by other established coach operators in Reading.

The Thackray's therefore put forward a mixture of trips to both seaside and other specific events. Coastal outings were to Lee-on-Solent and Hayling Island, whilst the popular circular tour to the New Forest was retained. Events covered were the two-day St. Giles' Fair held in Oxford, the Tidworth Military Tattoo, to Twickenham for Varsity and International Rugby Matches, to Wembley for the FA Cup Final, as well as all Reading Football Club away matches.

Some minor modifications were made to the existing excursions to Ascot and Epsom Races and the Aldershot Military Tattoo, whilst the tour to Brooklands had not proved popular and was deleted. The starting place for all excursions and tours was amended to the Colonnade as continued use of the Palace Theatre Parking Ground was now becoming uncertain due to a proposal to construct a new cinema on the site. All of the above licenses were approved on 21st April 1933.

Another annual local July event that attracted considerable crowds was the Henley Regatta, in particular the Saturday night with its fairground and fireworks display. As 'Thackray's' now had a service to the town, they naturally sought a license to enhance the service for that day. Only through passengers could be carried on the additional services, worked by two additional coaches sent from Reading.

Vera Thackray recalled that for her own excursions she like to go shopping at the London stores so conveniently served by the coaches. To this end she would ask her father for a free pass, but Bob would sometimes give her a hard time over such requests as he was 'careful' with his money.

A further enterprise was added from April 1933, though this time transport was not the theme! The 'Thackray's Fruit Stores (proprietor R. Thackray)' at No.3 Crown Colonnade marked the start of a new period of diversity. As well as the fruit stores, Bob was also active in getting building approval for some flats and offices elsewhere in London Road, Reading. Capitalising on that success, he had more built during the following year.

Thackray's hold on the Maidenhead to Henley road increased further from 28th July 1933, when they were granted a license for a service formerly operated by Harry Clinch of Maidenhead. The route left Maidenhead (Bridge) by way of the Bath Road and Thicket Corner, then onto Aston ('Flower Pot') via Knowl Hill, Warren Row, Crazies Hill, Cockpole Green, Kentons Corner, Remenham Hill, Henley (Market Place) and White Hill.

The above route improved links between Henley and the London service, and timetables advised passengers to change at the 'Pond House', on the Bath Road just to the east of Maidenhead, for the best connections. Shortly afterwards 'Thackray's' were successful in getting approval for a through fare between London and Henley.

As already highlighted, the viability of the Wokingham-Wargrave service as a feeder to the London coaches came under some doubt following the reduction in frequency. However, it did provide a useful link between the northern parishes of the Wokingham area and that market town. The route was further modified from August 1933 with an extension over the hill and along Blakes Road through Upper Wargrave to reach the Bath Road at Kiln Green. In doing so, the service took in a growing area of mainly Council housing, whilst it may have also been considered more appropriate for the terminus to be on the Bath Road as used by the London service.

It has been noted previously that a number of express coach operators were running over the road between Slough and London, so it is not surprising that the Traffic Commissioner decided to impose a set fare between those points with effect from July 1933. However, at the same time he upheld the protective fares imposed on services running over routes common to the Corporation's services within the Borough of Reading.

In August 1933 the fares between Newbury and Slough, Newbury and London and Maidenhead and London were also standardised with those of the long-distance services from Weston-super-Mare, Bristol and Cheltenham of the other operators using the Bath Road.

The additional spaciousness of the 'GP's was put to good use on the busy Reading-Maidenhead-London service, and GP5139 is seen soon after being acquired. This was just before fleet numbers were introduced, and only even numbers were used in order to give the impression that the fleet was larger than it actually was! The rather small route board is untypical.

The plight of London cabbies continued to cause concern, so much so that Sir Oswald Mosley and the Unionist Movement took the cause on as a rallying cry. Good support was found amongst the cabbies, though not those of Jewish origins. There were indeed many of that faith involved in the London cab trade, and during those difficult times the Thackrays were approached on a number of occasions with offers for their business.

With their income depressed yet further, London cabbies staged their most widespread strike from 2nd August 1933. The strike lasted for 12 days, and whilst 'Thackray's' had been little affected by previous disputes, that hit them as well.

Although it was owned by another operator, this fine preserved example of an Austin cab of 1935 typifies the type used for the 'Thackray's' fleet of the period. Most of this type lasted until c.1949.

Meanwhile local events in the Reading area were served throughout the year, one such example being the Woodcote Show of 7th August 1933. On that occasion the coaches ran a shuttle service between Pangbourne and the showground, where in fact Bob's daughter Vera was to be found adding yet more show-jumping awards to her growing collection!

THACKRAY'S WAY

Passengers please note the 7.30 p.m. coach from London to Reading is the last coach to catch the Newbury connection.

READING — NEWBURY

Reading to Newbury.					Newbury to Reading.				
Reading	Theale	Wool'ton	Thatcham	Newbury	Newbury	Thatcham	Wool'ton	Theale	Reading
A.M.	A.M.	A.M.	A.M.	A.M.	A.M.	A.M.	A.M.	A.M.	A.M.
655	710	724	735	750	750	8 5	816	830	845
855	910	924	935	950	955	1010	1021	1035	1050
1055	1110	1124	1135	1150	1155	1210	1221	1235	1250
1155	1210	1224	1235	1250	1255	110	121	135	150
1255	110	124	135	150	155	210	221	235	250
155	210	224	235	250	255	310	321	335	350
255	310	324	335	350	355	410	421	435	450
355	410	424	435	450	455	510	521	535	550
455	510	524	535	550	555	610	621	635	650
555	610	624	635	650	655	710	721	735	750
655	710	724	735	750	755	810	821	835	850
755	810	824	835	850	855	910	921	935	950
855	910	924	935	950	955	1010	1021	1035	1050
955	1010	1024	1035	1050	1055	1110	1121	1135	1150

Newbury — Reading .. 2/2 Return

Newbury — London .. 7/- Return

For intermediate fares see separate Fare Chart.

Children under 14 half fare.

Passengers are invited to apply for particulars of Season Tickets.

Timetable for the Reading-Newbury service issued April 1932.

106 During August 1933 Joseph Thackray passed away at the age of 89. However, more shocking for the family was the death at age 31 of Wilf ('Snips') Julian from septicaemia during July. Mr. Julian had originally been apprenticed at the Thornycroft factory in Basingstoke, duly becoming a Director of the family business. He was a popular and active man, with interests in amateur dramatics, car and motor-cycle racing. He was also credited with introducing the sport of motor-cycle football to Reading.

Throughout the Summer of 1933 the Company tried to get the Traffic Commissioner to allow inter-availability of return tickets between its own issues and those of 'Thames Valley' between Newbury and Reading. The latter opposed the idea, but in early December 1933 the measure was indeed enforced by the Commissioner.

However, the Thackrays found themselves beset by the loss of the Palace Theatre Parking Ground in late December 1933 as construction of the new cinema was due to start. Fortunately, some street works had already been undertaken about two years previous at Lower Thorn Street, when a lay-by had been formed to accommodate the 'Thames Valley' buses pushed out from St. Mary's Butts by the Borough Council. The latter authority therefore agreed to 'Thackray's' use of the facility, as before then the TV terminus had been transferred to Stations Square following the purchase of an interest in the latter concern by the 'Great Western' and 'Southern' railways.

The new location caused little inconvenience to passengers, being only some 50 yards from Cheapside, though it then meant that Thackray's movements could be clearly viewed from the nearby offices of 'Thames Valley'!

For the 1934 season of excursions and tours the Company sought to gain more patronage by the use of additional picking up points both within Reading and along the routes out of the town. Additional destinations were Marlborough Territorial Camp (in respect of the annual display in August) and the football grounds of Queens Park Rangers, Crystal Palace, Clapton Orient, Aldershot and Swindon in connection with Reading F C's away matches. All other existing excursions and tours were retained.

107 During September 1934 the Traffic Commissioners agreed to changes on the service taken over from Harry Clinch. The section back from Henley to the 'Flower Pot Inn' at Aston had been found to be uneconomic, so the terminus of the route was amended to the Market Place in Henley.

A further proposed development very close to the Colonnade site also had the financial backing of Bob Thackray, though in this instance he managed to keep his name out of it. An application was put forward by Mrs. A.L. Smith, licensee of the adjacent 'Marquis of Granby' pub, for permission to store and dispense petrol from No.124 London Road. The site was on the eastern flank of the pub grounds, and Bob had already replaced the previous building with a new single-storey shop-style property. Indeed, so advanced was the project that the hanging sign advertising the facility had already been painted by coach-builder Ted Franklin.

However, when the proposal for four petrol pumps and storage of 2000 gallons of fuel came before the Borough Council on 23rd November 1934, it was met by a petition from the numerous other filling station proprietors in the vicinity. The Council actually decided that the position of the pumps was outside the permitted building line, though no doubt it had been pressurised by the petition. With the venture thwarted, the new building became a florist shop, remaining as such ever since.

To the west side of the Colonnade shops stood a pair of quite substantial semi-detached houses, one of which was occupied by the appropriately named Dr. Gilford – though whether he had a cure for the tendency for coaches of that make to boil over is not known! These houses had also been acquired by Bob Thackray and were replaced in September 1935 by the 'Granby Cinema', the new luxurious entertainment venue for East Reading.

 Firestone Tyre's advert from 'The Commercial Motor' in 1933.

Chapter Thirteen A Change of Direction

In the eyes of the travelling public 1934 had passed by as a fairly uneventful year for 'Thackray's', partly due to the stability brought about by the Road Traffic Act. However, all was not well within the Company itself, and behind the scenes wheels had been set in motion to dispose of the coach operations.

One of the operators with which 'Thackray's' had been on good terms for some time was 'Red & White' of Chepstow. The latter's coaches had used the Colonnade Coach Station and both operators had agreed to make through bookings on each other's services. 'Red & White' had been busily buying up the competition on its various express routes into London, so they were a natural choice to approach regarding a possible take-over.

A meeting took place between the 'Red & White' management, Bob Thackray and Andre Guilmant during January 1934. R&W sought further particulars, which were provided later that month. However, the asking price of £65,000 was considered too high, so the offer was rejected by the R&W Board when it met on 16th February 1934.

Following this failed attempt to sell the 'Ledbury Transport' part of the business empire, Bob placed the matter in the hands of an agent, a Mr. C.L.H. Pierce of Langley, Birmingham. Pierce's brief was to find a suitable buyer and his commission was set at £1000.

Understandably the agent approached 'Thames Valley' some time during early 1935, but again the asking price was considered too high. Indeed, TV had only offered £25,000 for the business!

All of the excursions and tours, other than that to the Marlborough Camp, were again licensed. However, no significant alterations to any of the services took place during 1935.

However, an interesting regular 'service' was added to cover the period from 15th July to 11th August 1935, when a 'pea-picker's special' was run daily (when required) between Reading and Binfield Heath. The coach left

 Reading at 6.30am and returned around 6.00pm, the arrangement being that a charge of 30 shillings was made for the whole coach.

An attempt was also made in October 1935 to gain some licenses for excursions from Maidenhead. The proposal involved excursions to the horse racing at Northolt Park, Reading FC matches at Elm Park Reading and also to Hayling Island on Sundays between 1st June and 30th September. The coaches would start at 'The Bear Hotel' and additionally pick up at 'The Pond House' on the Bath Road west of Maidenhead.

Although there were vigorous objections from the local coach operators and 'Thames Valley', both the Northolt Park and Hayling Island licenses were granted. However, other events were unfolding, so these licenses were not in the end taken up.

A certain amount of industrial disharmony had been brewing in the road passenger transport industry as the '30's wore on and the depression caused wages to slip behind the cost of living. 'Thackray's' were not immune to this, and some stoppages occurred as a result. Any crews who had not worked were docked pay, and therefore something of a bad atmosphere had developed between the management and its employees.

Bob Thackray's forays into property development had shown him that there were perhaps easier ways to make money than transport, bearing in mind that once again legislation had effectively thwarted the potential for future expansion.

Not being satisfied with the results of his agent's attempts to sell the Company on his behalf, Bob approached his old allies 'Birch Bros.' of Kentish Town. That long established bus, coach and taxicab operator had also entered the world of express coach operation following restrictions that had affected its ability to expand bus routes in central London.

News of the negotiations with 'Birch' reached the ears of 'Tilling Transport Ltd.', another organisation with its roots in an old established London bus and cab operator. However, 'Tilling' had expanded its influence over provincial bus and coach operations through either directly setting up subsidaries or buying shares in others. By the latter means, it had duly become a substantial shareholder in 'Thames Valley', and it was that

 Company's Chairman Sidney Garcke who had alerted 'Tilling' over the sale.

Although the TV Board had previously turned down the opportunity to buy the 'Ledbury' company, 'Tilling' held the view that it must not go to another competing operator. They, therefore, approached the Thackrays over the matter, narrowly preventing the deal with 'Birch' from going ahead. Whereas TV had limited funds and various other shareholders to consider, 'Tillings' considered the matter as one of strategic importance.

The TV management and Board were of course kept informed as a deal was hammered out, as it had always been 'Tillings' intention that the daily management of 'Thackray's Way' would be placed in the hands of that Company. Such a move may also have been regarded as necessary to ensure that the Road Service Licence for the London route did not have to be exposed to possible objections from competitors. Indeed, TV's General Manager was authorised by the Board to ensure that an understanding was agreed with 'London Transport' that no objection to continued operation would be forthcoming.

And so, the 'Ledbury Transport Co. Ltd.', was sold and passed under the control of 'Thames Valley'. The share capital passed to 'Tillings' on 20th December 1935, although the date for transfer to TV operation was set for 2nd February 1936. The price paid was £68,000, though some £28,000 of that represented the garage and shop properties of the Crown Colonnade. 3,800 £1 shares were transferred over, with 1000 each coming from Bob, his brother Jim and Bob's son Fred, whilst the remaining 800 came from Bob's sister Lizzie.

As already noted, some animosity had recently developed between the Thackrays and their crews, and therefore Bob's method of informing them of the sale was both timely and characteristic of him. He visited the Colonnade Rest Room, where some members of the road staff warned him they 'would get him' (meaning that an all-out strike was being planned). His response was both swift and effective – he chalked a message up on the blackboard, which simply said 'thanks for the memories – you're all fired!'

'Tillings' had decided that the 'Ledbury Transport' company would be operated by TV as a separate concern, with re-charging arrangements between the two operators. Thus TV vehicles hired to work over the 'Ledbury' routes, or vice versa, resulted to payments being transferred between the two companies on a monthly basis.

The new 'Ledbury' Board consisted of George Cardwell (Chairman), F. P. Arnold, Sir James Milne, Sir Ralph Cope, R. F. Clayton, H. A. Short and C. D. Stanley, the combination of which ensured that the interest of both TV and 'Tillings' were upheld. Each of the Directors also received 100 shares in the subsidary company.

Day-to-day management issues, such as fleet maintenance, road service licensing and financial accounting were placed under the care of the appropriate TV Senior Managers.

As the services of 'Thackray's' General Manager were no longer required, Mr. Guilmant found new employment with 'Thatcham Road Transport Services', a haulage operator with roots back to the early post-Great War period, based in Thatcham, Berkshire.

However, the elimination of 'Thackray's' did not bring immediate joy to TV, as many headaches resulted from the efforts to maintain cover on the services. The fleet of Gilford coaches had been 'let go' somewhat in the lead up to the sale, resulting in 'stop notices' being posted on them during inspection by the Ministry official.

Over half of the 31 coaches were put off the road, creating something of a crisis in the TV fleet. In an effort to cover schedules, various service saloons and some coaches were temporarily transferred onto the Reading-Maidenhead-London service whilst an urgent overhaul programme got underway on the acquired vehicles. Amongst those used were a trio of Leyland 'Tiger' TS3 coaches 258-60 (GN 5145, GN 5139 and GN 5150), which under the former ownership of 'Premier' had competed with both TV and 'Thackray's' along the Bath Road at the height of pre-Road Traffic Act competition!

All drivers and conductors were officially taken over from 1st February 1936, by which time all ex-'Thackray' coaches were working from TV's depots, other than the four kept in London. The latter had been transferred

THAMES · VALLEY

TRACTION COMPANY Ltd.

As from the 1st February, 1936,
THE ROAD SERVICES
operated by
THE LEDBURY TRANSPORT
Co. Ltd. (Thackray's Way)
will be controlled by the
THAMES VALLEY TRACTION
Co. Ltd.

Inquiries and Correspondence relative to these services should be addressed to 83, Lower Thorn Street, Reading.

READING—LONDON

by Express Motor-Coach

Every Half-Hour

From 7.5 a.m. to 10.5 p.m.

except

7.35 p.m., 8.35 p.m., 9.35 p.m. week-days.

7.5 a.m.; 1.35 p.m., 2.35, 3.35, 8.35, 9.35 Sundays.

Day Return Fare - 4/6

Use this service for the West-End Theatres and Shops, and the Exhibitions at Olympia.

T. GRAHAM HOMER,
M.Inst.T.,
General Manager.
83, Lower Thorn Street,
Reading.

The 'Thames Valley' announcement in the local press.

 from their old Ledbury Mews West parking area to the Kings Cross Coach Station in Judd Street.

Shortly after the take-over an application was made to remove the 'Ledbury' element from the Reading-Newbury service, that route being a sole TV operation from then. However, on both that service and the Henley links, TV provided special through fares at less than the sum of the individual fares charged for each pair of journeys. The 'Ledbury' company was also granted permission from August 1936 to run extra journeys between London and Reading after the cessation of regular services in connection with special events, for which fares up to double the normal rate could be charged.

'Ledbury' no.4 (GP 5140) awaits departure in Bridge Avenue, Maidenhead for Henley in April 1937. Note the 'on hire' sticker in the front bulkhead.

TV's first year's experiences of operating the former 'Thackray' services had left it with some mixed feelings. Covering the services had been very difficult initially, whilst no capital had been forthcoming to make any immediate disposal of the Gilford coaches a practical proposition. However, the elimination of competition had brought some good results at a time when the company had economy uppermost on its priorities. The timetable on the Reading-Newbury route had been amended as a sole TV operation, with the result that overall mileage had been reduced by 14%.

The terminal point of the Reading-Kings Cross service was transferred from Lower Thorn Street to Reading Stations with effect from 7th September 1936. The service was an intensely worked operation, with 786,226 miles run in the fist 11 months of that year.

Seen inside TV's Maidenhead garage in April 1937 is 'Ledbury' Gilford no.52 (GF 6677) after being repainted in full TV coach livery. Note that TV evidently removed the luggage racks from the coaches during overhaul. The vehicle to the left is former 'Marlow & District' Karrier no.14 (KX 8482).

Quite a lot of private hire work had already been booked with 'Thackray's' before the take-over, so the TV coach fleet had a busy season, given that so many of the Gilfords were off the road. In respect of the latter, seventeen of them passed through the workshops during 1936. All were repainted in TV's standard red and cream coach livery, which was much lighter than the shade used by ‘Thackray’s’. ‘Thames Valley’ fleetnames were carried, but the old headboards were retained, though for some reason (or perhaps just in error?) those on the ‘GP’s’ were amended to include an ‘s’ after ‘Thackray’. Route boards were soon replaced with the style carried by TV’s coaches on the London route through Ascot.

The two Maidenhead-Henley routes had been given TV service numbers 16 and 17 and were no longer ‘Ledbury’ operations. The 16 ran from Maidenhead (Bridge Avenue) to Henley via ‘The Pond House’, Tittle Row, Littlewick, Knowl Hill, Warren Row, Craizies Hill, Hatch Gate, Kentons Corner, ‘The Four Horseshoes’ and Remenham Church, whilst the 17 ran also from Bridge Avenue to Henley but via ‘The Pond House’, Tittle Row, Temple Golf Course, Hurley, Warren Row turn, ‘The Four Horseshoes’ and Remenham Church. Both were operated from the Maidenhead garage, and evidently at times some of the former ‘Thackray’s’ vehicles based there were hired to cover those services as well.

However, the overall picture improved on that road with the purchase from A.E. Warwick of his Maidenhead (Clock Tower)-Boyne Valley-Tittle Row-Thicket Corner-Burchetts Green-Temple Golf Club-Hurley operation from 5th April 1936. The latter route became the 24a and the timetable actually included many ‘shorts’ to Burchetts Green. No vehicle changed hands, and TV worked it from the Maidenhead garage using one of the 1926 batch of Tilling Stevens single-deck buses whilst the services were being reviewed.

TV was not too happy about the two Maidenhead-Henley routes it had inherited. Both were regarded as weak from a traffic point of view, and from 11th July 1936 the 17 was re-routed through Burchetts Green, effectively also replacing the former ‘Warwick’ service. In an effort to make those services pay, smaller vehicles were operated on a one-man basis, presumably with buses selected from the ranks of those involved in other recent takeovers.

One result of the take-over was the acquisition of 21 ‘Setright Insert’ ticket machines, which were more modern than those previously in use by TV. Probably in the interest of avoiding confusion amongst the conductors, the machines continued to be used on the former ‘Thackray’s’ London route until its wartime in suspension in 1942, after which they were hired to ‘Aldershot & District’ for the duration.

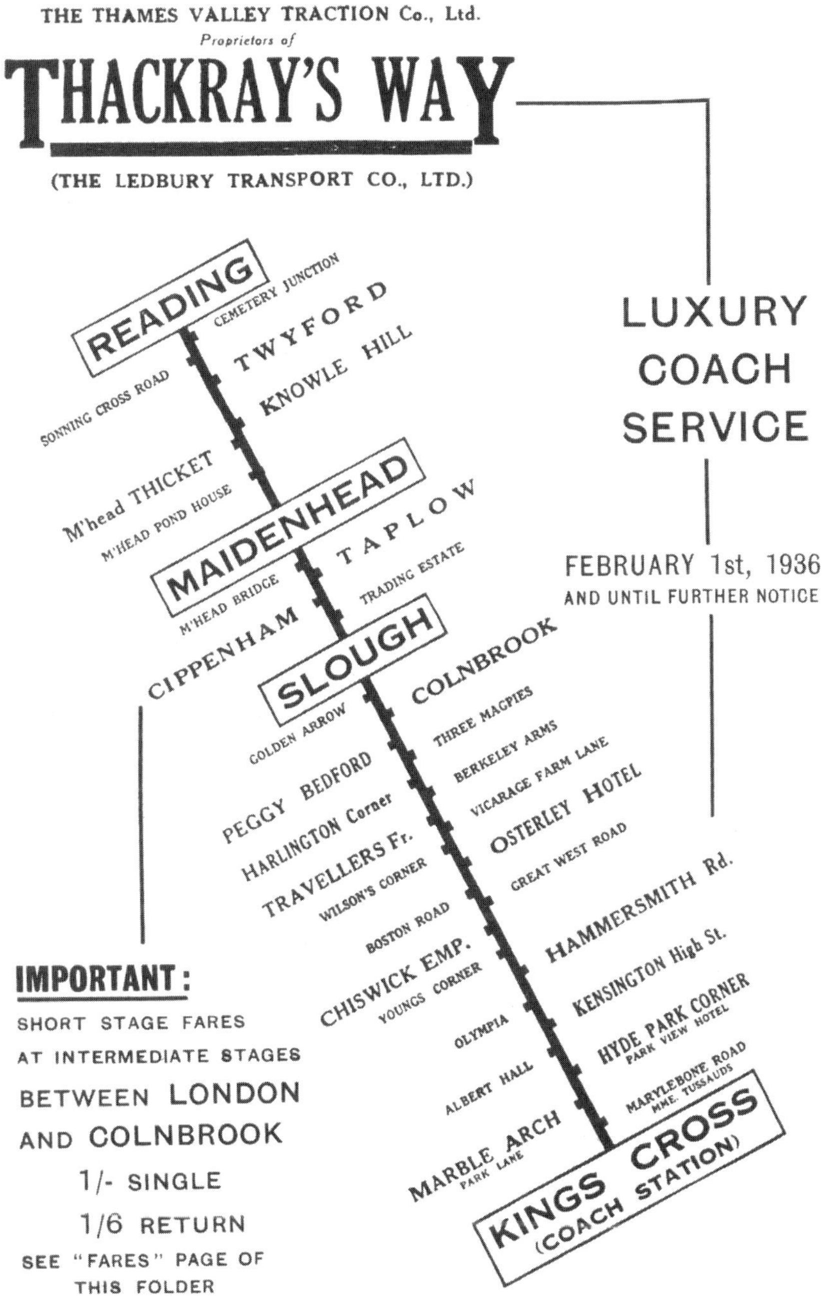
THE THAMES VALLEY TRACTION Co., Ltd.
Proprietors of
THACKRAY'S WAY
(THE LEDBURY TRANSPORT CO., LTD.)

LUXURY
COACH
SERVICE

FEBRUARY 1st, 1936
AND UNTIL FURTHER NOTICE

READING
CEMETERY JUNCTION
SONNING CROSS ROAD
TWYFORD
KNOWLE HILL
M'head THICKET
M'HEAD POND HOUSE
MAIDENHEAD
TAPLOW
M'HEAD BRIDGE
TRADING ESTATE
CIPPENHAM
SLOUGH
COLNBROOK
GOLDEN ARROW
THREE MAGPIES
PEGGY BEDFORD
BERKELEY ARMS
HARLINGTON Corner
VICARAGE FARM LANE
TRAVELLERS Fr.
OSTERLEY HOTEL
WILSON'S CORNER
GREAT WEST ROAD
BOSTON ROAD
HAMMERSMITH Rd.
CHISWICK EMP.
YOUNGS CORNER
KENSINGTON High St.
OLYMPIA
HYDE PARK CORNER
PARK VIEW HOTEL
ALBERT HALL
MARYLEBONE ROAD
MME. TUSSAUDS
MARBLE ARCH
PARK LANE
KINGS CROSS
(COACH STATION)

IMPORTANT:
SHORT STAGE FARES
AT INTERMEDIATE STAGES
BETWEEN LONDON
AND COLNBROOK
1/- SINGLE
1/6 RETURN
SEE "FARES" PAGE OF
THIS FOLDER

117 *The style of timetable cover adopted following the TV takeover.*

118 A curious postscript to the Thackray coach operations concerns the placing of an order, reputedly for 3 side-engined AEC Q-type coaches, not long before the sale of the company.

The AEC Q-type was a revolutionary design, with the engine position making the chassis ideal for modern-looking full-fronted coachwork. No doubt the Bournemouth-based ‘Royal Blue’ examples were frequent visitors to the Colonnade, but efforts to positively identify the ‘Thackray’s’ order for such chassis have produced only partial success.

What might have been! Artist’s impression of what a ‘Thackray’s Way’ AEC Q-type with Duple coachwork may have looked like.

What is for certain is that, on 4th January 1936, ‘Thames Valley’ found it necessary to pay £100 to Coaches & Components Ltd. of Holloway, London N7 by way of a cancellation fee for coaches on order.

Chapter Fourteen The Name Lives On

Following the sale of the Berkshire-based coach business, Bob was able to take a timely rest to pursue his involvement in Bowls. He had, for some time previously, played regularly at Reading Bowling Club, and he now had the chance to represent England in South Africa, sailing to there from Southampton on 3rd January 1936.

Left: Joe Thackray jnr. from a later Metropolitan Carriage Office Licence photo; right, Bob Thackray in riding gear about the time of his retirement.

The emphasis then shifted towards property investments, together with the continued operation of the cab fleet in London. The latter had already existed under the title of 'Robert Thackray Ltd.' since 6th January 1926, whereas the property business ran as 'Robert Thackray's Estates Ltd.'.

Not that the 'Thackray's' name had disappeared from its former routes as a result of the sale. Although 'Thames Valley' fleetnames appeared on the vehicle sides, and the legal ownership panel read 'The Ledbury Transport Co. Ltd., 83 Lower Thorn Street, Reading', all of the coaches retained the 'Thackray' signs fitted to the front of the roof. As the existing fleet numbers did not clash with the 'Thames Valley' series they continued to be used.

Publicity and timetables bore the rather cumbersome style of 'The Thames Valley Traction Co. Ltd., proprietors of Thackray's Way (The Ledbury Transport Co. Ltd.)'!

Having two Reading-London services did duly lead to the allocation of route numbers, though as was the case with most of the TV fleet, such numbers could not generally be displayed in the pre-war period! Rather than being given mere numbers, the status of the services was confirmed by the issue of letters instead. The 'A' was allocated to the service through Ascot, whilst the service via Maidenhead became the 'B'. There have been several suggestions regarding the choice of letters. On the one hand, the use of A for Ascot and B for the Bath Road has a certain logic to it. However, an alternative view was once quoted that the A was the first to be started (a for 'alpha', the first letter of the Greek alphabet), whereas that would place the B as 'beta', the second to start. Given the classical education enjoyed by the TV management of the day, the latter would seem equally plausible!

A postscript to the sale of the coach business occurred as late as February 1938, when the former agent decided to take Bob Thackray to court in a compensation case. It will be recalled that Mr. C.L.H. Pierce had been promised commission if he could successfully arrange for the sale of the Company in 1934. Although his approach to 'Thames Valley' had, as previously noted, been rejected, he endeavoured to link the subsequent take-over by TV with his efforts.

Amongst the witnesses called were Bob Thackray and George Cardwell, the latter being Chairman of 'Thomas Tilling Ltd.'. However, Pierce's claim was dismissed, as it was accepted that 'Tillings' had acted on its own initiative, and that the subsequent passing of operation to 'Thames Valley' was not connected with his earlier approach.

As already mentioned the Gilford coaches had to be retained by TV as no funds were available to replace them. Although the new 'Ledbury' schedules required far less vehicles, it was decided to maintain a fleet of much the same size as had been taken over. That was achieved by the transfer of vehicles from the main TV fleet as the Gilfords were disposed of steadily through the period 1937-1940. A separate summary gives full details, but it should be appreciated that most of the transfers were for 'book' purposes only, and is no indication that the vehicle ever ran over 'Ledbury' routes.

121 Some of the vehicles transferred, notably the Leyland Tiger TS7's were indeed regularly used on the London service, but were as likely to be found elsewhere 'on hire' to TV! At the same time certain TV vehicles, such as the dual-purpose batch of TS7's with sliding roofs, were often covering the London service 'on hire' to 'Ledbury.

'Thames Valley's' 1936 batch of dual-purpose TS7's were particularly involved with the 'Ledbury' company from late 1937. Some were actually transferred to the latter fleet, whilst others including car 306 (JB 8345) seen above, carried painted fold-down metal 'on hire to Ledbury Transport Co. Ltd.' plates fixed beneath the canopy. The full batch was 302-311 (JB 8341-8350), and full details of those transferred will be found in the fleet lists.

By February 1938 the Gilford fleet had been reduced to just eight examples, with only normal-control 62 (GJ 1332) and all of the forward-control batch 2-14 evens (GP 5139-5145). However, the London service was firmly in the care of Leyland TS7's, and the remaining Gilfords saw very little use except at busy times such as Bank Holidays, Ascot Races and Henley Regatta. All survived until being disposed of in April 1940.

The 'B' route continued to be the more heavily trafficked of the two London services throughout the pre-war and early wartime period. So much so that in May 1937 the Company was successful in getting approval to use double-deckers at peak times to avoid unnecessary duplication. No eye-witness reports have confirmed that such operation took place at that time, but the coming of the Second World War saw many additional persons in the area. In addition, there were parents coming to visit their children who had been evacuated to the relative safety of the Reading area. Double-deckers soon became the norm on the service until wartime restrictions brought a halt to express operations in November 1942.

During the war years a number of the Austin taxis were taken down to Fords Farm for storage as an air raid precaution. Although the Ledbury Mews West premises survived without a direct hit, there were numerous near misses as close by as the adjacent convent. Some of the cabs were taken for use as ARP fire tenders, but a number continued in service.

Like a ghostly apparition, these snow-dusted Austin taxis were caught by the camera from a window of the cottages in Ledbury Mews West.

Fords Farm had always been regarded as 'home from home' for various members of the Thackray family. Younger members recall with affection the gatherings of family, when all the children enjoyed the freedom of open space, the animals and the river and farm pond. The latter came into its own during the great freeze of 1943 when it froze over. Resident gardener Arthur Cox entertained the children by skating on the pond, and if they behaved he would pull them along on the ice! Accommodation was usually in the adjacent farm buildings, the old creamery having been converted. Later the loft was converted to accommodate George's family in order that they could have respite from the bombing, whilst other family members were there from time to time. A number of old horse-drawn 'Royal Mail' vans were on the site in use as chicken houses. However, by then there was no sign of any of the earlier generation of taxis or the remains of the Gilford coaches burnt in the Spencers Wood fire.

The final survivors of the once large fleet of Gilfords were the 'GP's. No.4 is seen here in Bridge Avenue, Maidenhead, with the Rialto Cinema behind.

Ben Thackray retired to Fords Farm during the Blitz, having always been a regular visitor there. However, during that period his wife died, so once peace returned he decided to go back to work at the age of 75. From then on he lived at the flat above the workshop at Ledbury Mews West.

Bob Thackray passed away in on 26th June 1950, some 30 years after he 'retired' to be a gentleman farmer in Berkshire. A colourful character in life, his widespread contribution to transport developments is still recalled by many former employees and passengers. At his funeral the mourners were so numerous that some 100 had to stand outside the church.

 The London cab business continued through the 1950's under the direction of Fred Thackray. Labour relations did, however deteriorate during that decade, with a particularly effective stoppage around the time of Queen Elizabeth's Coronation in June 1953. Indeed, the flags bought for decorating the taxis did not even come out of their boxes!

Newspaper photo of the striking cabbies of 1953, headed by the 'Thackray' drivers, accompanied by several of the Austin taxis.

As it was, there had nearly been another ending to the business during 1952, when a fire broke out in the workshop beneath rooms occupied by Ben Thackray. His grand-daughter Lily managed to alert him, whilst her father George stood between the fire and the petrol pumps with fire extinguishers until the fire brigade arrived.

In Reading TV had continued to use the Colonnade garage as a workshop to supplement the growing congestion at its Somerset Place garage. During 1938-9 the latter was rebuilt and greatly extended, so during that time some of the fleet was actually kept at the Colonnade. The coach station continued to be used by through services, and petrol sales and car parking also carried on as before, though they were suspended from 19th August 1940 to 7th January 1946 whilst the site was occupied by the Admiralty for the assembly of torpedoes. After peace returned, such activities recommenced, together with other uses such as the storage of crated Jeeps and use as a temporary garage for 7 tipper-lorries of the Reading Demolition Co., both of the latter occurring during 1946.

The 'Ledbury' coach service between Reading and London re-commenced on Saturday 17th May 1947, hopes of an earlier resumption having being dashed several times by shortage of manpower and vehicles.

The early post-war years saw an increase in activity at the Colonnade. This Bristol L6B coach 548 (FMO 23) was put on display when new in 1950.

126 With effect from 30th September 1947 the Colonnade became an operational base once again when some 20 vehicles, include a number of coaches, were garaged there. In December that year activity was further increased when a decision was taken to transfer some repainting work there to speed up the post-war refurbishment programme. Although some coaches continued to be based there for some years, operational use was gradually reduced over the next few years. The emphasis then changed to the use of the yard for storage of withdrawn vehicles, whilst the garage was used both for overhauls and the winter storage of coaches. A double-deck shed was built on part of the tea rooms site in 1953. It was put to good effect during the extensive body rebuilds undertaken by TV staff during both the 1950's and 1960's. The rest of the tearooms became the stores, part of which had been an bookings office until then, the latter being relocated at No.1 Crown Colonnade. It became common practice for a new coach to be displayed outside the coach station entrance each Spring, with suitable advertising material during the early post-war years.

TV finally applied to take over the licenses of the 'Ledbury Transport Co. Ltd.' in December 1949, after which the subsidary was finally wound up. All surviving members of the 'Ledbury' fleet resumed their former TV fleet numbers from 26th July 1950.

Although petrol sales and general parking had ceased with TV's operational re-occupation, the coach station continued in use by various through express services until the opening of the new bus station situated below the Top Rank Bingo Hall on 1st May 1967. Although the works remained in use, the level of activity inevitably declined after that.

To his son George's relief Ben Thackray finally retired from cab driving at 80, as his strength and powers of concentration were diminishing towards the end! He passed away in 1958, a very popular character amongst the cabbies and a link with a bygone era.

'Thackray' staff recalled at the London premises during the post-war period are:
George Weston, the mechanic who, after retirement, drove and maintained the seaside miniature railway at Hastings for some years.

A man known as 'Tyro' looked after the tyres of the fleet, who was so nicknamed due to his speedy wheel changes!

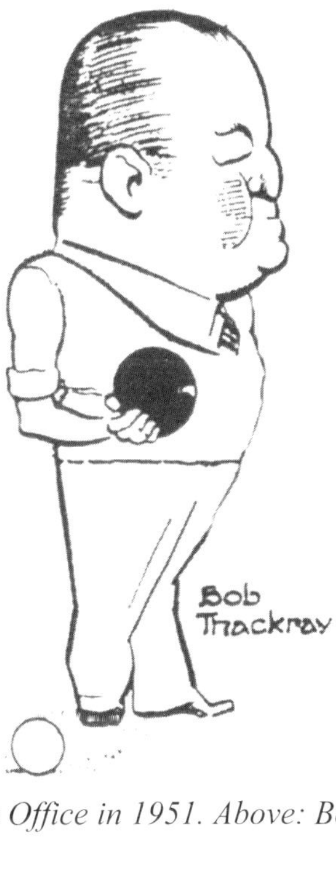

127 *Top: The Colonnade Office in 1951. Above: Bob Thackray bowling.*

 Other mechanics were from the Pugsley and Brown families and were related through marriage. A Mr. Butcher and Bill Witherington worked in the garage, the latter occupying the cottage nearest the arched entrance. Len Towner, who had originally worked for Cordery at Spencers Wood, was the person responsible for reading the incoming taximeters, which determined the takings to be paid to the drivers. Following the early death of his first wife, he met a girlfriend of George Thackray's wife Alice, married her and got himself transferred to London.

A character known as 'Deaffy' worked as night washer for the cabs, and his habits are recalled by Bob Thackray's grandson Stephen, who lived for a time in the mews. Firstly, he shouted at the cabs, or he would tie a chamois leather around a headlamp as if he was strangling someone! In reality he was gentle and simple in his ways, always keeping the cabs looking good.

Bob's daughter Edna had remarried Francis Saunders, but had tragically lost him to the Japanese after he returned early from a family holiday in Australia to Singapore just before it fell. He was interned in Changi Prison and later died from cholera contracted whilst working on the infamous Burma Railway. Edna and their son Stephen returned to England and both later became involved with the property business. Stephen spent much of his early years with his grandfather Bob and learnt much from him.

New cabs had continued to be purchased following the end of WW2, the later examples having diesel engines due to the high cost of petrol being a drain on profits. In order to cope with the maintenance of such engines Fred's son Brian was sent to learn how to maintain the injectors.

Brian actually left after a while to follow in his father's footsteps as a jockey, including several rides at Aintree. Later he took up saloon car racing and achieved some success in that, before settling down to horse-breeding. He also became the final family owner of Ledbury Mews West, later disposing of it for redevelopment, though many features still remain today.

However, in the second week of April 1959 Fred Thackray decided to sell the business. Some of the cabs were acquired by W.H. Cook & Sons Ltd., another long established cab operator of Huntsworth Mews NW1, whilst the remainder went to Mann & Overton, the dealers who had supplied the Thackrays with cabs through from the early days of the motor age.

129 Following the sale of the business, George Thackray finally learnt 'the knowledge' at 58 and drove his own cab until retirement.

And so, after nearly 90 years, the wheel had turned full circle, with just one member of the Thackray family driving a cab around the streets of London. But what an interesting and enterprising era it had been!

Tailpiece: Three proud Thackray brothers hold their hackney horses in the yard of Colville Mews in the early years of the 20th century, with Bob on left, Jim in the centre and Ben on the right.

Fl. No.	Reg. No.	Chassis Make/Model		Bodybuilder/Layout		Date New	Date Acq.	Date Out	See Note
16	UV 7962	Gilford	166SD	Duple	C26D	9/29	-----	4/37	A
18	UV 7963	Gilford	166SD	Duple	C26D	9/29	-----	4/37	A
20	UV 7964	Gilford	166SD	Duple	C26D	9/29	-----	4/37	A
22	UV 7965	Gilford	166SD	Duple	C26D	9/29	-----	4/37	A
24	UV 7966	Gilford	166SD	Duple	C26D	9/29	-----	3/37	A
26	UV 7967	Gilford	166SD	Duple	C26D	9/29	-----	4/37	A
38	UW 2615	Gilford	166SD	Duple	C26D	10.29	-----	9/36	A
40	UW 2616	Gilford	166SD	Duple	C26D	10/29	-----	4/37	A
48	UW 6646	Gilford	166SD	Duple	C26D	11/29	-----	4/37	A
28	UW 7597	Gilford	166SD	Duple	C26D	12/29	-----	4/37	A
30	UW 7598	Gilford	166SD	Duple	C26D	12/29	-----	4/37	A
32	UW 7599	Gilford	166SD	Duple	C26D	12/29	-----	4/37	A
34	UW 7600	Gilford	166SD	Duple	C26D	12/29	-----	4/37	A
36	UW 7601	Gilford	166SD	Duple	C26D	12/29	-----	4/37	A
---	MO 7526	Chevrolet	1-ton	?	B14F	4/26	12/29	*	D
---	MO 7924	Talbot		Andrews	C14F	5/26	12/29	*	D
---	MO 9039	Thornycroft	A1	Vickers	B20F	1/27	12/29	9/30	D
---	HO 6335	Thornycroft	BX	Vickers	B26R	9/24	12/29	9/30	DEF
---	OT 1339	Thornycroft	LB	Hall Lewis	B30R	5/26	12/29	4/30	DEB
---	RX 1456	Chevrolet LM	6whl.	?	B20F	3/28	12/29	9/30	DG
---	RX 1590	Chevrolet LM	4whl.	?	B14F	2/28	12/29	9/30	D
---	GC 1866	Gilford	168SD	Duple	C26D	1/30	-----	4/30	B
42	GC 1867	Gilford	168SD	Duple	C26D	1/30	-----	10/36	A
---	GC 1868	Gilford	168SD	Duple	C26D	2/30	-----	4/30	B
---	GC 1869	Gilford	168SD	Duple	C26D	2/30	-----	4/30	B
44	GC 1870	Gilford	168SD	Duple	C26D	2/30	-----	11/37	A
46	GC 1871	Gilford	168SD	Duple	C26D	2/30	-----	1/38	A
50	GF 6676	Gilford	168SD	Duple	C26D	4/30	-----	1/38	A
52	GF 6677	Gilford	168SD	Duple	C26D	4/30	-----	6/37	A
54	GF 6678	Gilford	168SD	Duple	C26D	4/30	-----	1/38	A
56	GF 6679	Gilford	168SD	Duple	C26D	4/30	-----	10/37	A
---	?	GMC		?	Ch20	c/24	4/30	10/31	HI
60	GJ 1331	Gilford	168SD	Duple	C26D	5/30	-----	1/38	A
62	GJ 1332	Gilford	168SD	Duple	C26D	5/30	-----	4/40	A
58	GJ 8024	Gilford	168SD	Duple	C26D	6/30	-----	by1/38	A
---	DP 3590	Dennis	30cwt	Vincent	Ch20	3/21	6/30	9/30	J
---	DP ?	Lancia		?	C20D	c/25	6/30	-/31	JL
---	DP 7669	Delahaye	83/59	Vincent	C20-	6/26	6/30	6/35	JK
---	VM 8638	Gilford	166SD	?	C26-	4/29	6/30	-/31	ML
---	RD 1886	Gilford	168OT	?	C30D	6/30	6/30	-/31	ML

Fl. No.	Reg No.	Chassis Make/Model		Bodybuilder/Layout		Date New	Date Acq.	Date Out	See Note
2	GP 5139	Gilford	168OT	Wycombe	C26F	7/31	8/32	4/40	AC
4	GP 5140	Gilford	168OT	Wycombe	C26F	7/31	8/32	4/40	AC
6	GP 5141	Gilford	168OT	Wycombe	C26F	7/31	8/32	4/40	AC
8	GP 5142	Gilford	168OT	Wycombe	C26F	7/31	8/32	4/40	AC
10	GP 5143	Gilford	168OT	Wycombe	C26F	7/31	8/32	4/40	AC
12	GP 5144	Gilford	168OT	Wycombe	C26F	7/31	8/32	4/40	AC
14	GP 5145	Gilford	168OT	Wycombe	C26F	7/31	8/32	4/40	AC

Notes:

A To Thames Valley Traction Co. Ltd. In 1/36, retaining Ledbury fleet numbers.
B Lost in fire at Cordery's Garage, Spencers Wood 24/4/30 whilst in store.
C Ex-Main Lines, London and Plymouth.
D Ex- Harold Cordery (Pride of the Valley), Spencers Wood. * These vehicles had been withdrawn before the takeover.
E Formerly Thornycroft demonstrators, (HO acquired 5/27, OT acquired 11/27).
F Became painter's store at Colonnade garage, Reading, finally sold 5/33.
G Became lorry with Ledbury. Body used as changing room at Ford's Farm, Calcot.
H Ex-Bert Ireland (Alexandra Coaches), Reading.
I Became Ledbury breakdown tender, sold 10/31, replaced by DP 7669.
J Ex-Edward Molesworth Hope, Reading.
K Became breakdown tender with Ledbury 10/31, finally sold 6/35.
L Sold to A. Andrews & Son (Favourite Coaches), Newbury without use.
M Ex-Charlie Tanton, Reading.

Note: *A fleet list for the* ***London buses*** *will be found at the end of the following appendix.*

Fleet Numbering:

Fleet numbers were not used until after the arrival of the ex-Main Line Gilfords in 1932. Only even numbers were used, in order to make the fleet appear larger than it was. The fleet list is arranged in the order that vehicles were delivered or acquired.

Service Fleet:

In addition to those former passenger vehicles noted above as becoming service vehicles with the Company, the following are recorded:

?? ???	Unic with pickup body	Ex-Thackray's taxicab	6/31	c.10/31
?? ???	Morris Oxford with van body	Reading runabout	10/31	5/36
TK ??	Morris Cowley 2-seater car	London Inspector's car	4/32	3/36

Taxi Fleet:

Unfortunately, as almost no official records or company records have survived for the taxi fleet, it has not proven possible to even attempt to construct a fleet list for that aspect of the Thackray family enterprises.

132 *'Pride of the Valley' MO 9039 was a Thornycroft A1 with a Vickers 20-seater, front-entrance body, new originally as a demonstrator in 1927. This vehicle was instrumental in causing the disastrous Spencers Wood fire in which it was a total loss, along with 3 brand new Gilford coaches.*

As the Gilfords were withdrawn, their places were taken by TV vehicles in what became a 'book' fleet. 'Ledbury' 18 (JB 7494) was a Leyland Tiger TS7 with Brush body new in 1935. It is seen during wartime at Oxford.

133 *The replacement No.36 (ABL 754) was this 1937 Leyland Tiger TS7 with Eastern Coachworks body, seen here at the Maidenhead bus station.*

TV's 320 (UR 3767), an AEC Reliance bodied by Craven of Sheffield, was originally in the fleet of the LMS Railway, coming to TV in 1936 from with the takeover of 'Chiltern'. It became 'Ledbury' no.60 for 7 months in 1938.

THAMES VALLEY TRACTION CO. LTD. VEHICLES TRANSFERRED TO THE LEDBURY TRANSPORT CO. LTD.

LT No.	TV No.	Reg. No.	Chassis Make/ Model	Bodybuilder/ Layout	Date New	Date Acq.	Date To L.	Date Out	See Note
18	238	RX 188	Thornycroft A2 L.	Chal. Ross B20F	5/27	3/31	12/37	1/38	A
52	352	VX 6549	Reo Sprinter	Duple B20F	6/30	6/37	12/37	7/38	F
20	300	RD 6270	ThornycroftArdent	? B26F	12/34	1/36	12/37	10/38	E
16	15	KX 8481	Karrier Coaster	Weymann B24F	4/32	-----	12/37	c.7/40	D
22	307	JB 8346	Leyland Tiger TS7	Brush DP32R	2/36	-----	12/37	5/38	
24	309	JB 8348	Leyland Tiger TS7	Brush B32R	2/36	-----	12/37	10/52	
26	310	JB 8349	Leyland Tiger TS7	Brush B32R	2/36	-----	12/37	8/50	
28	311	JB 8350	Leyland Tiger TS7	Brush B32R	2/36	-----	12/37	8/51	
30	321	ABL 751	Leyland Tiger TS7	ECW B32R	3/37	-----	12/37	10/52	
32	322	ABL 752	Leyland Tiger TS7	ECW B32R	3/37	-----	12/37	8/53	
34	323	ABL 753	Leyland Tiger TS7	ECW B32R	3/37	-----	12/37	8/53	
36	324	ABL 754	Leyland Tiger TS7	ECW B32R	3/37	-----	12/37	9/52	
40	325	ABL 755	Leyland Tiger TS7	ECW B32R	3/37	-----	12/37	8/53	
44	326	ABL 756	Leyland Tiger TS7	ECW B32R	3/37	-----	12/37	9/52	
48	331	ABL 761	Leyland Tiger TS7	ECW B32R	3/37	-----	12/37	10/52	
46	314	KX 7157	AEC Regal 662	Petty C32F	6/31	5/36	3/38	8/38	B
50	317	KX 6094	AEC Regal 662	Petty B32R	12/30	5/36	3/38	10/38	B
54	318	MY 639	AEC Reliance 660	Short B31R	10/29	5/36	3/38	10/38	B
56	257	UV 4080	Thornycroft BC	Vickers B26R	7/29	4/32	3/38	10/38	C
58	319	MT 1330	AEC Reliance 660	Hall Lewis B31D	11/28	5/36	3/38	10/38	B
60	320	UR 3767	AEC Reliance 660	Craven DP31R	6/29	5/36	3/38	10/38	B
18	294	JB 7494	Leyland Tiger TS7	Brush B32R	12/35	-----	5/38	10/51	
20	215	RX 5577	Leyland Lion LT1	Brush B29R	2/30	-----	11/38	3/50	
22	216	RX 5578	Leyland Lion LT1	Brush B29R	2/30	-----	11/38	2/50	
38	217	RX 5579	Leyland Lion LT1	Brush B29R	2/30	-----	11/38	3/50	
42	218	RX 5580	Leyland Lion LT1	Brush B32R	1/30	-----	11/38	2/50	
46	225	RX 6245	Leyland Lion LT2	Brush DP29R	7/30	-----	11/38	8/51	
50	226	RX 6246	Leyland Lion LT2	Brush DP29R	7/30	-----	11/38	4/50	
52	227	RX 6247	Leyland Lion LT2	Brush DP29R	7/30	-----	11/38	7/50	
54	228	RX 6248	Leyland Lion LT2	Brush DP29R	7/30	-----	11/38	3/51	
2	209	RX 5571	Leyland Lion LT1	Brush B29R	2/30	-----	4/40	2/50	
4	210	RX 5572	Leyland Lion LT1	Brush B29R	2/30	-----	4/40	2/50	
6	211	RX 5573	Leyland Lion LT1	Brush B29R	2/30	-----	4/40	2/50	
8	212	RX 5574	Leyland Lion LT1	Brush B29R	2/30	-----	4/40	2/50	
10	213	RX 5575	Leyland Lion LT1	Brush B29R	2/30	-----	4/40	8/50	
12	214	RX 5576	Leyland Lion LT1	Brush B29R	2/30	-----	4/40	2/50	
14	229	RX 6249	Leyland Lion LT2	Brush DP29R	7/30	-----	4/40	9/49	
62	230	RX 6250	Leyland Tiger TS3	Brush C29R	7/30	-----	4/40	7/40	

Notes:-

A Ex-E. & S. Keeps ('Rambler Coaches'), Burghfield Common.

B Ex'-Chiltern Bus Services', Lane End.

C Ex-'Great Western Railway', Slough.

D Originally in TV's 'Marlow & District' subsidary fleet, which had M&D fleet number.

E Ex-G. Jarvis & Son ('Reading & District Motor Services'), Reading.

F Ex-F. H. Crook ('Booker Bus Service'), Booker.

62 (RX 6250) was requisitioned by the military authorities. It was re-purchased by TV in 3/42, but reverted to the TV fleet with original number 230.

52 (VX 6549) this fleet number remains unconfirmed.

Vehicles remaining in stock after the liquidation of the Ledbury company reverted to their original TV fleet numbers from 26th July 1950.

Some dates out reflect final disposals, as during the early '50's a number of vehicles were de-licensed for some time and some were cannibalised for spare parts before sale.

VEHICLES OF ROBERT THACKRAY LTD. and JAMES D. THACKRAY

Fleet No.	Reg. No.	Chassis Make/Make	Bodybuilder/Layout	Date New	Date Out	See Note
4	XW 5667	Dennis 4-tonner	Dodson OT26/22ROS	12/24	10/27	P
1	XW 5668	Dennis 4-tonner	Dodson OT26/22ROS	12/24	10/27	P
	XW 5669	Dennis 4-tonner	Dodson OT26/22ROS	12/24	10/27	P
	XW 5670	Dennis 4-tonner	Dodson OT26/22ROS	12/24	10/27	P
3	XW 68	Dennis 4-tonner	Dodson OT26/22ROS	2/25	10/27	P
2	XX 906	Dennis 4-tonner	Dodson OT26/22ROS	2/25	10/27	P
5	XX 3882	Dennis 4-tonner	Dodson OT26/22ROS	3/25	10/27	JP
	YM 4719	Dennis 4-tonner	Dodson OT26/22ROS	1/26	10/27	P
	YF 5623	Dennis 4-tonner	Dodson OT26/22ROS	5/27	10/27	P

Notes:

J This vehicle was owned by James Deighton Thackray.

P All of the above were sold to the 'London Public Omnibus Co. Ltd.'. They were given 'Public' fleet nos. D85, D81, D82, D80, D83, D87, D86, D88 and D84 respectively.

136 *The more unusual of buses transferred to 'Ledbury' was this Karrier Coaster of 1932. No.16 (KX 8481) was originally no.15 in the 'Marlow & District' fleet. It survived the war, though where it was stored is unknown.*

TV's Leyland Lion LT1 214 (RX 5576) became 'Ledbury' no.12 in 1940. It is seen here in the 1947 floods at Maidenhead, after a bodywork rebuild.